◀ 世界汉语教学学会名师讲座系列 ▶

Teacher's Development
and TCSOL

教师发展
与国际汉语教学

英汉对照

（英）西蒙·博格（Simon Borg） 著
和静 赵媛 译

外语教学与研究出版社
FOREIGN LANGUAGE TEACHING AND RESEARCH PRESS
北京 BEIJING

图书在版编目 (CIP) 数据

教师发展与国际汉语教学：英汉对照 / （英）西蒙·博格（Simon Borg）著；
和静，赵媛译. —— 北京：外语教学与研究出版社，2018.6（2019.7 重印）
（世界汉语教学学会名师讲座系列）
ISBN 978-7-5213-0115-1

Ⅰ. ①教⋯ Ⅱ. ①西⋯ ②和⋯ ③赵⋯ Ⅲ. ①汉语－对外汉语教学－师资培养－
研究－英、汉 Ⅳ. ①H195.3

中国版本图书馆 CIP 数据核字 (2018) 第 137381 号

出 版 人　徐建忠
责任编辑　张立萍
责任校对　鞠　慧
装帧设计　姚　军
图片摄影　姚　军
出版发行　外语教学与研究出版社
社　　址　北京市西三环北路 19 号（100089）
网　　址　http://www.fltrp.com
印　　刷　北京九州迅驰传媒文化有限公司
开　　本　650×980　1/16
印　　张　9
版　　次　2018 年 7 月第 1 版 2019 年 7 月第 3 次印刷
书　　号　ISBN 978-7-5213-0115-1
定　　价　45.00 元

购书咨询：（010）88819926　电子邮箱：club@fltrp.com
外研书店：https://waiyants.tmall.com
凡印刷、装订质量问题，请联系我社印制部
联系电话：（010）61207896　电子邮箱：zhijian@fltrp.com
凡侵权、盗版书籍线索，请联系我社法律事务部
举报电话：（010）88817519　电子邮箱：banquan@fltrp.com
物料号：301150001

记载人类文明
沟通世界文化
www.fltrp.com

出版说明
Publisher's Note

　　随着"汉语热"的不断升温,汉语教学和汉语应用的全球化趋势日益明显。截至 2017 年 12 月 12 日,全球已有 146 个国家和地区建立了 525 所孔子学院和 1113 个中小学孔子课堂。其中,"一带一路"沿线有 53 个国家设立了 140 所孔子学院和 136 个孔子课堂。然而,在国际汉语教学快速发展的同时,我们也面临着许多问题和挑战。例如,国际汉语教师人数相对不足,师资队伍建设有待进一步加强;本土化教材开发亟待新的突破;高效可行的教学方法急需被探索等。在诸多挑战之中,教师发展问题又成为重中之重,直接决定了教学的质量与效果。在这样的背景下,教师研究方兴未艾。其以教师为主导,以学校为基础,以实践为导向,以持续为特点,能够培养教师的反思意识,调动他们的工作积极性,并最终提升教学水平。

　　针对国内和国际教学的现状,世界汉语教学学会于 2017 年夏季特别举办了"国际汉语教师培养与发展高级讲习班"。此次讲习班特别邀请到英国利兹大学的 Simon Borg 教授，这是他首次为国际汉语教师作讲座。针对目前教师发展面临的困境，他简要概括了教师职业发展研究的现状、方法和步骤，介绍了教师研究的关键特征和研究技巧，对怎样进行高质量的语言教学研究进行了深入的探讨。很多教师和研究者慕名而来，并就汉语教学中的问题与 Simon Borg 教授进行了积极的互动。

　　Simon Borg 教授的讲座非常具有启发性、实践性和学术价值。应许多参会教师的要求，在征得了 Simon Borg 教授同意之后，外研社国际汉语出版中心以 Simon Borg 教授的两场讲座内容为素材，精心推出了《教师发展与国际汉语教学》一书。本书主要有以下特点：

　　1. 呈现方式：本书改变了传统学术书籍的纯英文版或纯中文版呈现方式，中英文并排的形式使本书便携、易懂，更适合国际汉语教师和学生深入理解教师发展与职业研究新理念，帮助大家节省查阅工具书的时间，提高研读效率。

　　2. 选材来源：英文以 Simon Borg 教授的两场讲座内容为原材料，考虑到不偏离其语言风格和讲座的整体流畅性，全稿英文在修订过程中保留了个别口语片段表达。中文主要来自现场的同声传译材料，同传译员为北京外国语大学孔子学院工作处和静副处长和高级翻译学院赵媛老师。本书编辑修改了口译材料中的一些口误、重复、语法等问题，将材料进行了一定程度的语言书面化加工，整体上内容取材于现场讲座，所以中文和英文都偏向口语的语言风格，亲切易懂。

3. 立体性阅读体验：读者可通过扫描封面二维码或登录封面上提供的网址获取现场讲座视频，深入感受现场讲座及交流气氛，加深对本书内容的理解。

最后，希望本书可以为广大国际汉语教师及研究生、第二语言教学研究者和对国际汉语教学感兴趣的人士提供帮助，帮助大家深入理解教师发展研究领域的新理念，并最终应用到教学实践中。

外语教学与研究出版社
国际汉语出版中心

目录
Contents

序言

　　本书汇集了我 2017 年 7 月在北京举办的"国际汉语教师培养与发展高级讲习班"上所做的两场讲座的内容。我能够参加这次活动源于外语教学与研究出版社（FLTRP）的大力支持，对此我表示衷心的感谢。

　　在第一场讲座中，我们讨论的主题是教师职业发展研究。这是当今全球教师发展模式中的一个重要问题，近年来在外语教育中的作用也日益突出。人们越来越意识到，传统的自上而下和短期的教师职业发展模式并没能像预期的那样，在教学和学习上产生持久、有意义和积极的改变。因此，近年来许多研究的重点更多地放在了以教师为主导、以学校为基础、以实践为导向的持续的职业发展模式，从而有可能在教学和学习方面产生更持久的变化。教师研究就是可供教师们选择的方向之一。它涉及教师们在自身课堂进行系统性探究的过程。通过教师研究，教师可以找出那些他们想要探索的、与工作相关的问题，决定最佳的探究方向，在课堂上开展小规模调查，并利用研究成果调整教学方式。教师研究是一个严格的反思过程，教师可以单独进行，但如果合作完成，效果会更好。教师研究的目的是职业发展；这是与学术研究不同的最主要的一个方面，因为学术研究的目的是产出与该领域更普遍相

Preface

This volume brings together two lectures I gave at a seminar on foreign language teacher development in Beijing in July 2017. My participation at this event was facilitated by the Foreign Language Teaching and Research Press (FLTRP), whose support I warmly acknowledge.

In the first lecture we addressed the theme of teacher research for professional development. This is an important issue in contemporary approaches to teacher development globally and has also become increasingly prominent in foreign language education in recent years. There is growing recognition that traditional top-down and short-term models of teacher professional development do not provide the kinds of lasting, meaningful and positive changes to teaching and learning that are anticipated. As a result, there has been much emphasis in recent years on more teacher-led, school-based, practically-oriented and ongoing forms of professional development which have the potential to lead to more sustained changes in teaching and learning. Teacher research is one such option available to teachers. It involves teachers in the process of systematic inquiry in their own classrooms. Through teacher research, teachers can identify issues of relevance to their work that they want to explore, decide on how best to investigate them, conduct small-scale inquiry in their own classrooms, and use what they learn to adjust how they teach. Teacher research is a rigorous reflective process that teachers can do individually but which is enhanced when it has a collaborative dimension too. The purpose of teacher research is professional development; this is one key way in which it differs from academic research, where the goal is to generate

关的知识。

第一场讲座中，在简单介绍了有效的职业发展后，我们定义了教师研究的关键特征，概述了教师研究过程的步骤，指出了教师研究的优势和不足，并在研讨会的最后提出了一系列建议，从而促使教师研究对教师、学生和学校都更有效和有益。

第二场讲座更加概括地看待了整个研究过程，并回顾了外语教学研究者能够用来提高工作质量的步骤。质量是研究中的关键问题，与研究过程的所有阶段——计划、实施和报告都有关联。在这一讲中，我们主要关注研究的计划和实施。

在任何关于研究质量的讨论中，一个重要的着手点就是定义"研究"。教师要避开那些过于狭隘的定义，也不应偏爱特定类型的研究，因此在讲座早期确立的定义侧重于在各种研究中都很重要的要素，例如精心的计划、系统的实施以及数据的收集与分析。然后讨论定量和定性研究之间的区别，并阐明混合方法研究的价值。

研究的质量很大程度上会受到计划阶段决策的影响，包括各种需要考虑的问题，以及如何提高质量的建议。什么是高质量的研究课题？评估研究问题的质量需要使用怎样的标准？好的文献综述的特点是什么？如何使研究符合伦理？这些是我们重点讨论的几类问题。

研究过程中的一个关键元素是收集数据，这也是该讲座关注的问题。其中一个关键问题在于，研究人员面临很多选择，选择适合研究问题的研究方法尤为重要。我们重点关注了问卷调查，因其在外语教育研究中被广泛使用。讲座中还说明了一个更普遍的观点，即我们使

knowledge that is of more general relevance to the field.

In this first lecture, following a brief introduction about effective professional development, the key characteristics of teacher research are defined and the steps in the teacher research process are outlined. Benefits and criticisms of teacher research are identified, and in the final part of the session a series of suggestions are made which can make teacher research a more productive and rewarding experience for teachers, students and schools.

The second lecture looks at the research process more generally and examines the steps foreign language education researchers can take to improve the quality of the work they do. Quality is a key issue in research and it is relevant at all stages of the process – planning, implementation and reporting. In this lecture we focused mostly on the planning and implementation of research.

An important starting point in any discussion of research quality is defining what "research" is. It is important to avoid definitions which are too narrow and which favour particular kinds of research, and the definition established early in the lecture thus focuses on elements which are important to all kinds of research, such as careful planning, systematic implementation, and data collection and analysis. The distinction between quantitative and qualitative research is then discussed and the value of mixed methods research noted too.

The quality of research is significantly affected by decisions that are made during the planning stage and various issues that need to be considered are covered, with advice on how to improve quality. What is a good quality research topic? What criteria can be used to assess the quality of research questions? What are the characteristics of a good literature review? How do we make research ethical? These are examples of important issues that are discussed.

A key element in the research process is collecting data and this is also an issue that the lecture focused on. One key point is that many options are available to researchers and it is important to choose research methods that are appropriate given

用的每种研究方法总会存在优点和缺点。

为了总结第二场讲座，我们提供了一份清单，包含提高语言教育研究质量的九条建议。这些建议将有助于研究人员计划、实施并报告其工作成果。

每次演讲结束后，都会有一个问答环节，这一部分也包含在本书中。

再次感谢外语教学与研究出版社（FLTRP）使本书得以出版。

西蒙·博格

2018 年 4 月 16 日

the research questions that are being addressed. We focused in particular on questionnaires, as these are widely used in foreign language education research and the discussion illustrates the more general point that there will always be advantages and disadvantages for every research method we use.

To conclude this second lecture, a list of nine suggestions for improving the quality of language education research is provided. These will be of value to researchers as they plan, conduct and report the results of their work.

After each lecture there was a question and answer session, and the contributions to these have also been included in the volume.

I would like to thank FLTRP again for making this publication possible.

Simon Borg

16 April, 2018

教师职业发展研究

介绍

　　本讲内容由三部分组成：首先，介绍职业发展的不同方法；其次，集中介绍作为职业发展策略的教师研究；最后，是大家的交流互动环节。首先我来简要介绍一下我自己。

　　我很多年前就开始做教师，但从来没有教过英国学生英语，而是教其他国家的学生学习英语这门外语。大概做了十年的英语教师后，我进入高校做师资培训的工作，1998 年开始侧重学术研究，在利兹大学做了十五年科研。最近五年，我在外语教师职业发展领域做顾问。所以我今天主要讲的是职业发展，尤其是职业发展的一些策略，我们可以将它们运用在自己的工作当中，即教师研究。

Teacher Research for Professional Development

Introduction

This session will be divided into three parts. In the first part I will talk about different approaches to professional development. In the second part I will focus on teacher research as a strategy for professional development. Then in the final part you will have the opportunity to ask any questions you have. But first I will say a few words about my background.

I started off my career many years ago as a school teacher and I taught English as a foreign language (always outside of the UK). I worked as a school teacher for about 10 years, and then I also became a teacher trainer. In 1998 I moved into academic career and worked for 15 years at the University of Leeds. For the last five years I have been working as a consultant in the area of professional development for foreign language teachers. And this is the focus of today's session – professional development generally and one particular strategy for professional development that you can also use in your work – teacher research.

职业发展的方法

首先，先谈一下对职业发展的方法的整体认识，分三点来说。

1. 职业发展至关重要

首先，大家肯定都同意这个观点，即职业发展至关重要，对于所有教师而言都是如此。这其实是没有任何争议的。作为一名教师，如果不考虑职业发展，就意味着你的事业经过一段时间后会变得非常无聊，做的事情都是重复性的。职业发展可以让我们一直对自己的工作保持一定的新鲜感，从而不断进取，不断寻找工作中的新挑战。所以，职业发展能够让我们的工作变得非常有意思、令人兴奋，而且非常具有挑战性。没有职业发展，我们的职业生活就会变得非常无聊，变得有一点可悲，只是在进行重复性工作。

2. 全球活动发展显著

第二个观点，放眼全球，职业发展的速度是很快的。真的很快。我们到每个国家都会看到一些教师在做职业发展，有很多活动，这特别好。也就是说，不同的组织或国家部门都认识到了职业发展的重要性，他们给予教师很多机会来不断拓展知识、强化技能，所以进展是相当可观的。我觉得中国也是这样，中国的外语教师无论是教汉语，还是教英语或其他语言，都有很多机会参与职业发展。实际上这种职业发展的机会并不少，对全球的外语教师来说都是如此。

3. 影响有限

我的第三个观点有一点批判性和消极。如果看一下职业发展在全球范围内产生的影响，根据我所掌握的情况，这种影响还是很有限的。我的意思是什么呢？职业发展的目标不仅是给教师提供新知识、新技能，还要让教师能够把这些知识、技能应用到实际教学中。这是职业发展的最终目标，也就是要改变和改进教师在课堂上的教学行为。在我看来，这才是职业发展的目标，不仅要提供知识，而且要让教师能够把知识运用到实践中，更有效地进行教学，从而帮助学生更有效地学习。所以，当我讲到职业发展的影响比较有限

Approaches to Professional Development

Let's start off with the overall argument I'd like to make. There are three parts to this argument.

1. Professional development is vital

First of all, I don't think we can disagree that professional development is vital for all teachers. There is nothing controversial here really – without professional development you will find that your career can become quite boring and repetitive. Professional development is necessary to keep us excited about our job, to keep us moving forward, to keep us looking for new challenges. Therefore, professional development keeps the job interesting, exciting and challenging. Without professional development, our lives as professionals can become a bit boring, a bit sad, and a bit repetitive.

2. Global activity is significant

The second point is that, if we look around the world, there is a lot of professional development taking place. A lot. Every country I visit, I see examples of teachers doing professional development. There are plenty of activities, which is good. It means organisations and ministries recognise the importance of professional development. They are giving teachers lots of opportunities to further their knowledge, their skills. That's all very positive. I think in China, it's no different. Teachers in China, foreign language teachers, whether it's Chinese or English or other languages, have a lot of opportunities for professional development. There is no shortage of opportunities for professional development for foreign language teachers around the world.

3. Impact is modest

My third point is a bit more critical and negative. If we look at the impact of all this professional development around the world, my feeling is that its impact is modest. What do I mean by that? The purpose of professional development is not just to give teachers new knowledge or new skills. But it is for teachers to take that knowledge and to take those skills and to use them in their teaching. This is the purpose of professional development ultimately. It's to change and to improve what teachers do in the classroom. That for me is the purpose of professional development. It's not to give teachers knowledge for the sake of it. It's for teachers to use that knowledge to teach more effectively. And therefore to help students

时，我的意思是说我们常常看不到教师职业发展为课堂教学带来什么变化。教师可能学到了更多的知识和新的观点，但并不一定能够给课堂教学带来变化。对我来说这是一个问题。如果说课堂教学行为没有发生变化，为什么还要花这么多财力、物力促进教师职业发展呢？

几年前，Guskey（2000，p.3）写道："职业发展的文献里充斥着关于过去失败的描述……对于现代职业发展课程的评论经常是悲观的。"这些评论在今天仍然有效。换句话说，职业发展项目没有带来期望中的影响，并未真正发挥作用。这是对全球职业发展现状的客观评价。很多政府对职业发展都进行了大量投资，但是在学校、教室里几乎没有产生任何变化。对我来说这是一个严肃的问题。

这是我的总体观点，我相信职业发展非常重要，它在全世界范围内也取得了很大进展，但还没有对教学产生应有的影响。原因之一是，也许教师参与的职业发展活动的类型不是最有效的。我现在给大家进一步解释一下。

这是一段来自中国教师的话，他表达了在中国参加职业培训课程的一些感想：

> 我参加了两门在职培训课程。我觉得这些培训对教学没有用处……（每门培训课程）仅持续了一周……所有教师坐在一间大教室里，听发言人在讲台上讲理论。他们的理论听起来非常深刻，但是，大部分听众都听不懂这些理论。（Li，2015）

大家注意，这位教师说自己参加了两门在职培训课程，注意不是一门，是两门，可见机会挺多的。但是他接着说："我觉得这些培训对教学没有用

learn more effectively. So when I say that the impact of professional development is modest, what I mean is that, very often, we don't see any change in the classroom as a result of professional development. We know teachers have more knowledge. We know teachers have learned new ideas. But we don't necessarily see anything changing in the classroom. For me, this is a problem. If things are not changing in the classroom, why are we investing so much money and so much effort in professional development for teachers?

Several years ago Guskey (2000, p.3) wrote that "the literature on professional development is filled with descriptions of past failures... and reviews of modern professional development programmes are often just as pessimistic". These comments remain valid today. In other words, professional development projects very often do not have the hoped-for impacts. This is a realistic assessment of what's happening around the world. Governments invest a lot of money in professional development but little changes happen in schools and classrooms. For me this is a serious issue.

So this is the overall argument I want to start with today. I believe that professional development is important. There is a lot of it happening around the world. But it doesn't have as many impacts on the classroom as it should. And one explanation for that is because the kinds of professional development teachers take part in are not necessarily the most effective kinds. I will explain that now as we go along.

Here is a quotation from a Chinese teacher who was reflecting on their experience of taking part in a professional development project in China.

> I participated in two in-service training programmes. I think they are useless for my teaching... (Each course) lasted only one week... with all the teachers sitting in one large classroom and listening to the lecturers talking about theories. Their theories sounded profound but most of the audience did not understand them. (Li, 2015)

As you can see the teacher said "I participated in two in-service training programmes". Not one, but two, so opportunities are available. But he said "I think they are useless for my teaching..." These are the teacher's words, not mine. The teacher was being asked about the effect of the training on their teaching. And this is one of the things he said. "I think they are useless for my teaching." And then he explained more, "(Each course) lasted only one week." This is often the problem. Courses are short. "with all the teachers sitting in one large classroom and listening to the lecturers talking about theories. Their theories sounded profound but most

处……"这是这位教师说的，不是我说的，这是我们采访教师们培训感受时他的反馈。他觉得培训对教学没有用，因为"（每门培训课程）仅持续了一周"。培训时间太短，这常常也是问题所在。"所有教师坐在一间大教室里，听发言人在讲台上讲理论。他们的理论听起来非常深刻，但是，大部分听众都听不懂这些理论。"

对全球许多教师来说，故事都是相似的：参加一个培训班，坐在那儿，一直听，然后回到自己的学校，还是一成不变地按照原来的方法教学。所以职业培训的影响有限确实是个严肃的问题。

我们看到两难的境地：职业发展至关重要，但通常又没有效果。我们看到了充满矛盾的两个方面，所以我的职业使命就是帮助解决这个矛盾，使职业发展更有效。如果我一定要总结一下今天的目标，就是设法使职业培训对教师起到更大的作用。

培训模式

我们来看一下存在的障碍。为什么职业发展不能奏效呢？其中一个原因就是职业发展的模式，或者我们称之为培训模式。大家可能对培训模式这个说法比较熟悉，因为这可能是世界上最普遍的模式。大家可以看到这种职业发展培训模式有四个特点。下面我们逐一进行讨论。

外部定义

首先，它是外部定义的。"外部定义"的意思是所有关于培训的决定，比如说培训什么（即教师要学什么）、怎么学、什么时候学，都不是由教师决定的，而是由其他人决定的。教师并未参与决策，这是个问题，因为如果教师没有参与决策，那么他们参与培训的动力会非常低。

不知道是否有人被迫参加职业发展课程。当你被迫做一件事情的时候，你学习的动力就不会很强。因为你知道这并不是你真正想做的事。教师经常被要求参加一些职业发展的活动，而他们并未对这些活动的设计和内容做出过任何贡献。这个因素会限制职业发展的效果。事实上，许多职业发展的一个问题是："需要知道那些新知识是由教师群体之外的某个人来确定的。"（Muijs et al. 2014，p.247）

我在全世界范围内见过许多这样的例子，一个教育机构决定教师需要进

of the audience did not understand them."

For many teachers around the world, this is a familiar story. They attend courses. They sit there. They listen. And they go back to their classroom, and they continue doing what they were doing before. So I think there are serious questions here about the impact of professional development on what teachers do.

This becomes a paradox, a contrast, a contradiction. On the one hand, professional development is important. But, on the other, professional development is very often ineffective. We have got these two ideas going different directions. One of my professional missions is to try to make a small contribution to addressing that problem, to try to make professional development more effective. If I have to summarise the purpose of my work professionally today, that's what my purpose is, to try to make professional development a bit more effective for teachers.

The Training Model

Now let's think about some of the obstacles, some of the barriers. Let's think about why professional development is very often not so effective. One explanation is that the professional development model that is followed is what we called a training model, and you will be very familiar with this, because this is the most common model around the world. There are four characteristics of this training model of professional development and I will go through these now.

Externally defined

First of all, it's externally defined. By "externally defined" I mean that all the decisions about the training, decisions about the content (what the teachers will learn), decisions about how teachers will learn, about when teachers will learn, all the decisions about the training are made not by the teachers, but by other people. There is no teacher involvement in decision making. That can be a problem, because if teachers are not involved in the decisions, sometimes teachers can be less motivated to participate.

I don't know if you've ever been forced to attend a professional development course, if you've been told "you must attend this course". When we are forced to do things, of course sometimes our motivation is not very high, because it's probably not what we really want to do. Teachers are very often required to take part in professional development activities whose design and content they have

一步学习一个特定话题。然后所有教师不得不学习，但是这些话题通常并不是教师想要学习的东西。这就会成为一个问题。

输入为主

职业发展模式的另一个特点是以输入为主。重点在于输入。换句话说，就是教师坐那儿听，很多情况下，教师参加职业培训，就是坐在那儿听。现在大家想想，如果在自己的教室里面，教学生外语，那么输入是不是最好的一种教学方法呢？换句话说，如果他们一直坐着听你讲，这是一种好的教学方法吗？当然不是了。这不是以学生为中心的教学方式。但我们的教师培训经常采用这种方式。让教师坐在那里听培训课程，即使我们知道这样的方式对学生也不是很好。我并不是说通过工作坊或讲座给教师增加输入不好，问题是输入通常是教师有机会获得新知识的唯一途径。以输入为主的职业发展有以下特点。我们逐个讨论一下。

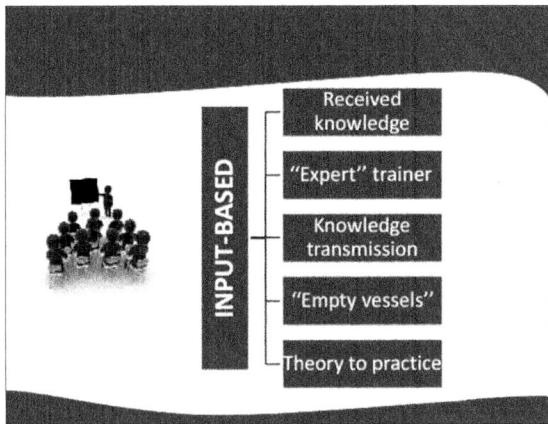

• 知识已知

教师体验的很多职业发展方式是输入式的，这种模式更强调所谓的"已知知识"。已知知识指的是来自外部，如书本、理论、研究的一些知识。其他类型的知识包括基于经验和实践的知识。这种知识叫作实践知识，它也很重要，但是培训强调的更多的是已知知识。

• "专家"培训师

在教学过程中，通常会有一个所谓"专家"的培训师。有意思的是，很多职业发展项目当中的"专家"，本身是一个培训师。但是教师们呢，教师

not contributed to. This is a factor which can limit the impact that professional development has. In fact, one problem with much professional development is that "the need to know something new is identified by someone external to the group of teachers" (Muijs et al. 2014, p.247).

I see many examples around the world where an educational authority decides that teachers need to learn more about a particular topic. And then all the teachers have to study it, but very often that's not what the teachers want to learn. That can be a problem.

Input-based

Another characteristic of this approach to professional development is that it's very input-based. The focus is on input. In other words, the teachers sit and listen. Very often teachers go to teacher training workshops and they sit and listen. Now if you think about teaching students in your classrooms, if you think about teaching students foreign languages, is input the best way for them to learn? In other words, if they sit in your classes and listen to you speaking all the time, is that the best way for them to learn? No. We agree that it's not a very learner-centred way. But yet when we teach teachers, that's the way we very often teach them. We make them sit and we make them listen even though we know that's not very good for our students. I am not saying that giving teachers input through workshops or lectures is bad. The problem is that very often input is the only way in which teachers have opportunities to acquire new knowledge. Professional development that is input-based has several features which you can see in the next slide. I will now comment on each of the points here.

• Received knowledge

In an input-based approach, there is a lot of emphasis on what we call "received knowledge". Received knowledge is knowledge that comes from external sources, from books, from theory, from research. There are other kinds of knowledge that come from experience, that come from practice. So we can also talk about practical knowledge. That's important, too. But very often in training, the emphasis is on received knowledge.

• "Expert" trainer

When professional development is input-based, there is always an "expert" trainer. It's very interesting that in a lot of professional development the "expert" is the trainer, but what about the teachers? Are our teachers not experts in their own classrooms? You are much more expert than I am in doing what you do. I cannot do what you do as well as you do. So the idea that the trainer is the expert and the teacher is something else is, for me, problematic. We need to recognise that the

们不是专家吗？他们不是课堂上的专家吗？在你们所在的专长领域中，你们比我强得多，我肯定无法和你们相比，我不是你们这个领域的专家。所以，在培训领域，专家和教师是脱节的，而这是有问题的。我们必须要认识到教师本身也有很多不同类型的技能，而且必须要利用这一点进行培训。

• 知识传递

在输入型职业培训中，知识传递是重点。知识很重要，但是更重要的是如何利用知识，使教学更加高效。而这一点在职业发展培训模式中往往是缺失的。教师被灌输了知识，但是没有学到如何使用它们。

• "空罐子"理论

还有一个"空罐子"的概念。"空罐子"指的是一个空空如也的容器，里面什么东西都没有。这是一个隐喻，用来比喻教学。如果我们把学生看作空罐子的话，我们就假设他们不能把知识带入学习过程中，他们不是空着手，而是脑子里面空空如也。这种情况在培训过程中经常发生。我们把教师们看作空的容器，把教学重点放在灌输知识上，而不是利用他们已有的知识充实教学过程。

• 从理论到实践

关于培训模式的最后一点是它假设理论是第一位的，理论会影响实践。换句话说，教师会学习一些理论，将这些理论应用到课堂教学中，所以理论指导实践。有的时候这是正确的，但是这并不是完全正确的教学方法。这不是我们教学的方式。作为教师，我在教学过程中，最先想到的不是某个理论以及将这个理论运用到教学中。我会先考虑其他事情，比如课程设置和学生，比如我昨天或者上周讲的内容，等等。除了理论，还有很多事情会影响教学。所以认为教师学习就是将理论应用于课堂教学的想法是有问题的。

总的来说，在职业发展培训中，主要依靠为教师提供来自外部"专家"资源的知识输入是存在问题的。

短期培训

职业发展培训面临的另一个问题是短期培训。一周的课程，半天的研讨会，一个小时的研习班，即使是一天的工作坊也很难对教师的课堂教学带来多大的改变。某一天你可能有一些新的想法，但是很难带来实质性的改变。因此我们需要更长时间的职业发展培训。

teachers have a lot of expertise, a different type of expertise. We need to use that to support professional development.

• **Knowledge transmission**

In an input-based approach to professional development there is also a lot of emphasis on knowledge transmission, giving teachers knowledge. Of course knowledge is important. But it is also important to help teachers use that knowledge to teach more effectively. This is often missing in a training model of professional development. Teachers are given knowledge but they receive no support in understanding what to do with it.

• **"Empty vessels"**

There is also this idea of "empty vessels". An empty vessel is a container that has nothing in it. It's empty. This is a metaphor for teaching and learning. If we treat learners like empty vessels, we assume that they bring nothing to the learning experience. They come, not empty-handed, but empty-headed. This can often happen to teachers in training courses. We treat them as empty vessels. And we focus on giving them knowledge through input rather than also trying to use the knowledge they already have.

• **Theory to practice**

One final characteristic of input-based professional development is that it assumes that that theory comes first and will then influence practice. In other words, teachers will learn some theories, and then they will go away and apply them in the classroom. The theory does influence practice some of the time, but that's not the way teaching generally works. That's not the way we teach. In other words, when I am planning a lesson, I don't start by thinking of a theory and then trying to apply it to my lesson. I'm thinking about lots of other things. I am thinking about curriculum. I am thinking about my learners. I am thinking about what I taught yesterday, or last week. There are a lot of things happening that influence teaching, not just the theory. So the idea that teacher learning is the process of applying the theory to the classroom is problematic.

Overall, then, there are problems with the approach to professional development that relies mainly on providing teachers with input from external "expert" sources.

Short-term

Another problem with a lot of professional development is that it's short-term. A one-week course, a half-day seminar, a one-hour workshop. A one-hour workshop, even a one-day workshop, is not really going to lead to many changes in what teachers are doing in the classes. In one day, you will get some new

关于短期职业发展培训，我想说明三点。

• 一次性工作坊（"肇事逃逸"）

教师们经常参加一次性的工作坊。我们有时称之为"肇事逃逸"的工作坊。在英语中，"肇事逃逸"指的是发生交通事故，比如说两车相撞时，本应该负责的司机撞完就跑，逃之夭夭。我们用这个词来描述这样的职业发展：一个培训人员来了，快速做了一次研讨就离开了，和教师们再无任何联系。不时会有人邀请我到他们国家去做一个这样的工作坊，我也并没觉得这是在浪费时间。但我们必须客观看待它们在教师身上所能产生的影响。通过工作坊，教师可以获得一些新的理念，但是单独的一次工作坊不会使教师的行为产生重要的长期改变。人们已经做了一些研究，来探讨工作坊产生的影响。研究显示，"工作坊在改善教师教学方法以及学生表现方面的效果非常糟糕"（Gulamhussein，2013，p.3）。

• 单一事件 vs. 过程

短期培训把职业发展当作一个单一的事件。然而，职业发展是一个持续性的过程。教师的职业生涯很长，理想状态的职业发展会持续很长时间。这是一种我们需要通过教师体会职业发展来提升的观念。弄清楚职业发展是一个单一事件还是一个过程很重要。

• 效果与时间有关

研究表明，职业发展持续时间越长，影响越大。关于持续时间没有统一的观点，但普遍认为教师需要多次持续获得这种机会来掌握新知识、新技巧，并把它们成功地应用到教学中。所以，你在这方面花费的时间越长，效果越好。但这并不是让你每天进行职业发展培训，一直持续六个月。我的意思是你要定期、持续地做这件事情，这比在短期内进行密集培训的效果要好得多。

与实践脱节

最后一点是，很多职业发展的培训模式都是与实践脱节的。教师的大部分时间都花在了学校教学上。那里是职业实践发生的地方。但是，当教师需要学习的时候，他们却要去其他地方。这很有意思，我认为学校是最佳的学习地点，所以教师的职业发展与教学通常是脱节的。这就好比两座房子，我们在左边的房子里进行教学，在右边的房子里进行职业发展，这两者之间没有任何联系。如果这两者能够建立紧密联系的话，效果就会大大提升。

The Constructivist Model

In contrast to the training model described above, a constructivist model of professional development has the following characteristics and I will now discuss these.

Participant-centred

First of all, it's a much more participant-centred model. For example, in a constructivist model, teachers are involved in some of the decisions about what to learn and when to learn it and how to learn it. I will provide some examples of this below.

Ongoing

A constructivist model of professional development sees teacher learning as a process not an event. It therefore employs strategies which can unfold over time rather than short-term or one-off activities. Loucks-Horsley et al. (2010, p.11) talk about "the need to shift professional development from one-time workshops to more ongoing and job-embedded professional learning".

Situated

The training model above was criticised for not being closely connected to what teachers do in the classroom. In contrast, a constructivist approach is situated. It locates teacher learning within the context of teachers' daily practices. Teachers I meet around the world often say to me, "A lot of the training we do is too theoretical." When they say that, they don't mean it in a positive way. They are not saying, "We love it because it's theoretical." What they mean is that "I couldn't make any connection between the training and what we do. It wasn't practical enough". A constructivist approach seeks to address such concerns so that teachers feel that professional development is relevant to their work and builds on their experiences and knowledge. Zepeda (2015, p.3) says that "job-embedded learning is the ticket to supporting teachers as they engage in the complexities of their work".

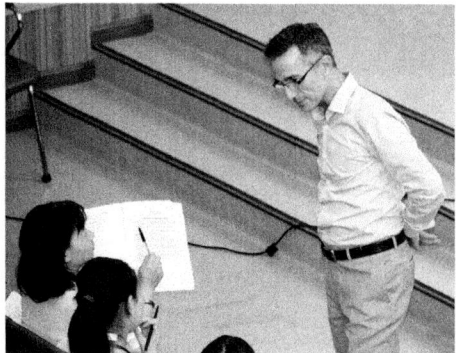

Zepeda (2015，p.3) 说："嵌入式学习是一张门票，可以帮助教师参与到这种复杂的工作中。"

社会化

社会化也是建构主义模式的一个特点，这里的"社会化"指的是我们鼓励教师共同学习和相互学习。教师们也有能够相互分享借鉴的专长。外部支持仍有发挥的空间，但"专家培训师"不再是知识的唯一来源。教师同样知识渊博，他们可以通过分享知识进行学习。Johnston (2009，p.241) 指出："当教师能够一起学习的时候，便能够以一种可持续性的，而且是有意义的方式进行职业化学习。"所以职业发展被视作一种社会活动。

基于探究

建构主义模式的最后一个特点是强调探究，它是教师学习的重点模式。探究是非常重要的。你进行职业化的学习，同时探究你自己的学习过程，而不是让别人给你灌输教学知识。根据 Burton (2009，p.300) 的观点，"好多教师都认为反思是职业发展中的重要工具"。基于探究的职业发展鼓励教师通过基于论证的策略来进行学习。我们将要详细讨论的教师研究，就是基于探究的职业发展策略的一个例子。我们可以把反思的实践者作为教师的几种比喻之一，如下所示。

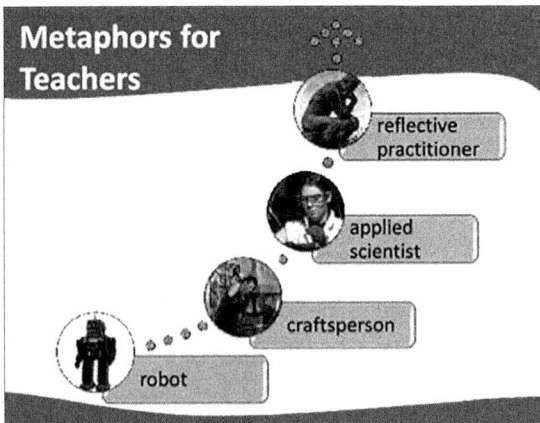

Metaphors for Teachers
- reflective practitioner
- applied scientist
- craftsperson
- robot

• 机器人

在最底部，我们可以看到，它把教师比作机器人。机器人是很机械的。机器人不会思考，仅仅按照写好的程序去行动。机器人不会做决定。它有没

Social

Social is another important characteristic of this constructivist approach to professional development. By "social" we mean that teachers are to learn together and from one another. Teachers have expertise that they can share and which other teachers can learn from. There is still room for external support, but the "expert trainer" is not seen as the only source of knowledge. Teachers, too, are seen to be knowledgeable and they learn by sharing that knowledge. Johnston (2009, p.241) says that "teachers can only learn professionally in sustained and meaningful ways when they are able to do so together". Professional development is thus seen to be a social activity.

Inquiry-based

One final point here is that in a constructivist model there is an emphasis on inquiry as a key mode of teacher learning. The idea of inquiry is very important. You learn professionally by reflecting and investigating your own teaching, not simply by listening to someone else talking about teaching. According to Burton (2009, p.300), "most teacher educators would argue that reflection is an essential tool in professional development". An inquiry-based approach to professional development encourages teachers to study their work via evidence-based strategies. Teacher research, which we discuss in detail later on, is an example of an inquiry-based professional development strategy. We can think of the reflective practitioner as one of several metaphors for teachers, as shown below.

• **Teacher-as-a-Robot**

At the bottom we have the teacher as a robot. A robot is mechanical. And a robot doesn't really think too much. A robot is programmable. A robot does what it's programmed to do. Robots don't make decisions. Do robots have emotions? No. Maybe that's one good thing about machines. But of course you are a teacher, emotions are important. So there are many reasons why the metaphor of a robot is not a good one for teachers. If you feel like a robot, you probably will feel your job is not very fulfilling, exciting or rewarding. But very often teachers are

有感情呢？没有。可能机器的优点就是没有感情。但是对于教师来说，情感是很重要的。因此，机器人这个比喻实际上对于教师来说并不是一个准确的比喻。如果你觉得自己像机器人，你很可能会觉得你的工作毫无成就感，无法令你振奋而且没有价值。但是很多情况下，在培训教师的时候，我们就把教师当成了机器人。我们告诉教师怎么做，希望他们完全按照我们所说的方式去做，同时也没有给他们机会让他们自己做决定。我们不给他们自主性。如果教师有时有一点儿不高兴，我们还会觉得很意外。但事实上，这并不令人意外。

• 工匠

另外一个比喻是把教师比作工匠。工匠制造东西，有的工匠做珠宝，有的工匠用铁或金属进行制作，比如铁匠。他们的双手非常灵活，擅长使用工具，所以这是一项技术工作。但是，用工匠形容教师合适吗？可能不是特别合适。其中一个原因是，工匠工作没有什么高深的理论，因为这份工作完全是从实践出发的。怎么成为一个工匠呢？需要看书吗？很可能不需要。你不断向师傅学习，然后模仿他们，慢慢就变成了工匠。这是成为一个好工匠的途径，也就是向师傅学习，这就是一种学徒制。你不断模仿大师的作品，向他们学习。在教学当中我们也通过观察资深教师来进行学习。我们可以看看他们是怎么教的。但是，我确定"模仿"这个词用得很准确，因为教学背后还需要很多思考。你不能只是单纯地模仿。这种比喻的另外一个问题是，工匠的学习模式非常传统。正因为每一个新的工匠都在模仿大师，所以他们的作品并没有太大变化。我模仿我的师傅，而我的徒弟又会模仿我，这种传统会保持很长时间。可能会突然出现一个才华横溢的人打破这种传统，但是总的来说，工匠这个行业是比较传统的。工匠这个比喻与教师有一些联系，但是没有非常有效地抓住教学的内容。

• 应用科学家

第三个比喻是把教师比作应用科学家。应用科学家做什么呢？应用科学家研究理论，然后应用理论。但他们不是单纯的科学家。科学家创造理论，但应用科学家研究理论并付诸实践。在教学中两者的确有相似的地方。教师需要学习一部分理论。但是教学不仅限于此，不只是把理论应用到教学当中，它还包括更多的东西。所以我们说应用科学家和教师，或者和职业发展，其

treated like robots. We tell teachers what to do. We expect them to do it exactly the way they are told. We don't expect them to make independent decisions. We don't give them any autonomy. But then we are surprised that teachers feel a bit unhappy sometimes. Well, it's no surprise at all.

- Teacher-as-a-Craftsperson

The next metaphor for teachers is the craftsperson. So the craftsperson makes things. Someone who makes jewellery. Someone who makes things out of steel or metal, like a blacksmith. They are very skilled with their hands. They are skilled in using tools. It is a skilled job. But is it a suitable metaphor to describe the teacher? Maybe not. One reason is that being a craftsperson is a very practice-based activity. In other words, how can you become a craftsperson? Do you study books? Probably not. You become a craftsperson by working alongside with experts and imitating what they do. That's how you become good at a craft. By working alongside an expert. It's kind of a practice model. You learn by imitating. In teaching, we can learn by observing more experienced teachers. It's good to see what more experienced teachers do. But I'm sure that imitating is the right word, because there is a lot more thinking behind teaching. You don't just imitate people. The other problem with the idea of teacher as a craftsperson is that it's a very conservative model. In other words, because each new craftsperson imitates the master, things don't really change very much. I do what my master does. And when I become a master, the next generation will imitate me. Things stay the same for a very long time. Occasionally there will be someone who does things differently. But generally this is quite a conservative model. It has some relevance to teaching, but does not capture very effectively what teaching and learning involve.

- Teacher-as-an-Applied scientist

The next metaphor is the teacher-as-an-applied scientist. What does an applied scientist do? An applied scientist studies theories, and then applies them. They are not pure scientists. The pure scientist creates the theories, but the applied scientist studies the theories and applies them. There is some of that in teaching because we do learn and use theories. But teaching is more than that. Teaching is not just about applying theory. There is more to teaching. So again, the applied scientist model has some relevance to teaching, to professional development. But it doesn't go far enough, because teaching is not just about studying a theory and applying it. I'm sure you've studied many theories, and I'm sure when you've taken these theories to the classroom, some of them have worked and many of them haven't. So it's not enough to learn the theory. You have to take it to the classroom. Very often you have to experiment with it and you have to modify it on the basis of our experience.

实有一定的相似之处，但是还不够深入，因为教学不仅仅是学习和应用理论。我想大家肯定都学过很多理论了。我也相信，大家在教学当中也会发现有一些理论是奏效的，但是有很多理论并没有太大作用。因此光学习理论是不够的，我们必须要把理论带到课堂中。我们需要进行验证，不断地修改和调整。

- 反思的实践者

要做到这一点我们必须学会反思，这就是最后一个比喻——反思的实践者。其实这种对于教学的描述算是最现代的观点。教学确实是需要一些技艺的，因为我们需要技巧来进行实践。但是我们也需要学习理论并应用它们。同时我们还要记住，我们需要进行非常深入的反思才能做好教师。我们需要思考我们要做什么，需要对自己的工作进行评估。自己的教学是否有效？如果有效是因为什么？无效又是因为什么？我怎样在下一次进行补救？会反思的教师就会问自己这些问题。而应用科学家、机器人和工匠都是不会进行反思的。在建构主义模式中，这些是至关重要的。

总结：今天的职业发展

我之前说过，很多证据表明，我们应该减少对于带有上述特征的职业发展模式的依赖。这个模式是由外部因素决定的，是短期的、以灌输为主的，没有考虑到实际情景。这个模式很难为课堂教学带来改变。

我们需要怎么做呢？我们需要更加强调以教师为主导。换句话说，我们要给予教师更多做决策的机会。职业发展需要持续更长时间，而且要以思考、探寻和反思为驱动，同时还要考虑到不同的情景。此外，我们还要考虑到不同的社会因素。这样的话，培训才能够更有效，对于教师、学生和学校来说，收获才会更大。

这是几个职业发展策略的例子，它们具备

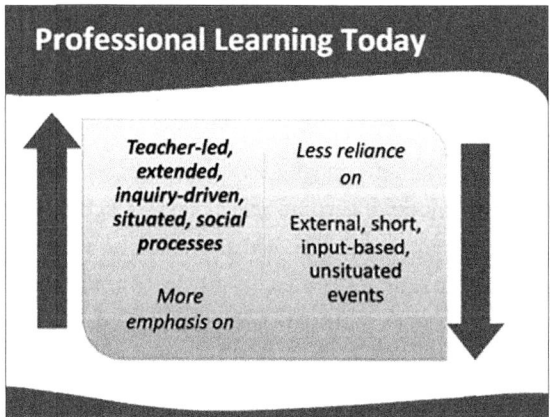

Professional Learning Today

Teacher-led, extended, inquiry-driven, situated, social processes

More emphasis on

Less reliance on

External, short, input-based, unsituated events

• Teacher-as-a-Reflective practitioner

And to do that we have to reflect, which is the final metaphor we have here, the metaphor of the reflective practitioner, which is the most contemporary way of thinking about teaching. So teaching, yes, there is a lot of craft to it, because we need to learn to do something practical. There is a lot of applied science to it, because we need to learn theories and use them. But we also need to remember that there is a strong reflective component of being a good teacher, because we need to think about what we do, and we need to evaluate what we do. Did it work? Did it not work? Was it effective? If it wasn't effective, why wasn't it effective? If it didn't work, why not? How can I make it better next time? These are the kinds of questions that the reflective teacher asks. The applied scientist, the craftsperson, certainly the robot don't ask these kinds of questions. These are the kinds of questions that are essential for the constructivist model of professional development.

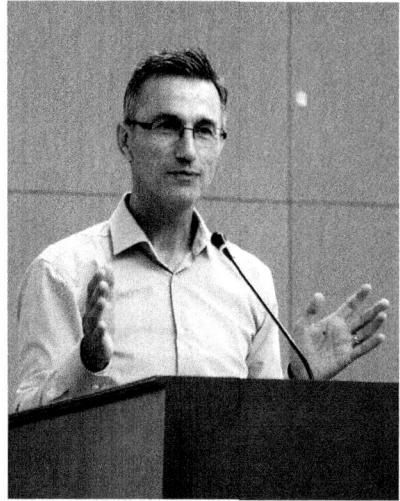

Summary: Professional development today

Based on what I've said so far, we can conclude that to improve the impact of professional development we need to rely less on approaches which are based on externally-defined, short, input-based, unsituated events. Professional development that has those characteristics will have less impacts on teaching and learning in the classroom.

On the other hand, teacher development is likely to be more effective when it is teacher-led, in other words, when teachers are involved in decisions; when professional development is extended, and takes place over time; when it's inquiry-driven, with focus on reflection; when it's situated and social. When it has all these characteristics, professional development for teachers is likely to be much more effective and much more rewarding not just for teachers but also for their learners and schools.

Here are examples of strategies for professional development that reflect some of those positive characteristics that I've talked about. These are approaches to professional development that have these characteristics. They are teacher-led,

了我刚才所讲的一些优点。积极的职业发展具有这样的特点：它是以教师为主导的、社会的、情景的、持续进行的，等等。我们来看几个例子。当然，我稍后会着重介绍教师研究，但大家可能会对其他几个方法感兴趣，所以我来简单说说其中几个。

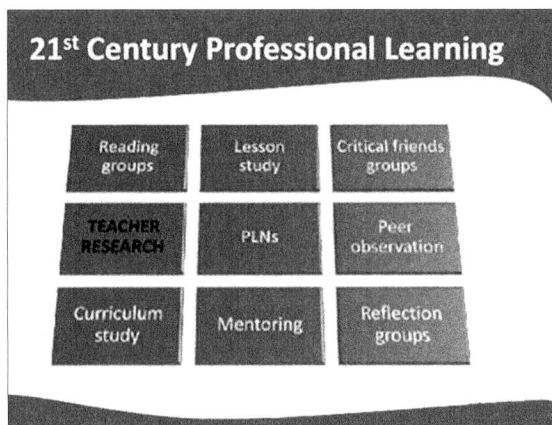

阅读小组

阅读小组是职业发展里一个非常简单的概念。同一所学校或几所附近学校的教师，可以建立这样一个阅读小组，进行面对面交流。什么时候在哪儿见面，由教师来决定。他们为什么要见面？因为他们要讨论一些他们都读过的东西。那么谁来决定读什么呢？由教师自己决定。所有的决策都由教师自己来做，教师自己决定见面时间、交流时长、见面地点以及阅读内容。这和另外一种模式是完全不一样的。那种模式由别人来做所有决定，并告诉教师必须要做什么。而这种模式赋予了教师一种责任感。教师可以选择阅读内容。教师不能说这个和我没有关系，因为所有阅读材料都是教师自己挑选的。他们可以在学校见面，或在校外见面。他们可以创造一个很轻松的氛围，可以一周或者一个月见一次，这都是教师自己决定的。关键是他们可以有规律地这样做。

课程学习

课程学习也是需要合作的。课程学习相当于备课。通常来讲，教授同一年级或同一门课程的教师坐在一起共同备课。他们一起进行课程教学的规划。他们说："下星期我们将在六班上第三单元，现在我们一起来规划一下。"这

social, situated, on-going, etc. Let's look at a couple of them. Of course, the one I'm going to talk in more detail about is teacher research, but I'll just very briefly comment on some of the others in case you are interested.

Reading groups

Reading groups is a very simple idea for professional development. We have groups of teachers, who normally work in the same school or maybe nearby schools. And they meet. When do they meet? The teachers decide. Where do they meet? The teachers decide. Why do they meet? They meet to discuss something that they have all read. Who decides what they are going to read? The teachers. So you can see the decisions here are in the hands of the teachers. The teachers decide when to meet, how long to meet for, where to meet, and what to read. This is very different from an approach where someone else makes all these decisions and tells the teachers what to do. This approach gives teachers more responsibility for their own learning. The teachers will choose something they want to read that is connected to their teaching, so the work they do will also be relevant. Teachers can meet at school; they can meet outside of school. They can make it a formal meeting; they can make it an informal meeting. It's really up to the teachers. They can meet once a week; they can meet once a month. It's up to the teachers. The idea is they do this regularly.

Lesson study

Lesson study again is collaborative. In other words, a group of teachers work together. Normally it's a group of teachers who teach the same level or course or grade. What they do is that they plan the lesson together. They sit down. They say, "Right, next week we are teaching Unit 3 to Class 6. And we are going to sit down and we are going to plan this lesson together." They do it collaboratively. They look at the objectives, the activities and the resources. It's a collaborative planning exercise. Then one of the teachers will teach that lesson. One. The other members of the team will attend the class as well and observe it. While the teacher is teaching, the others are observing closely and making notes about what's happening. In particular, what the observers focus on are the students. They pay close attention to what the students are doing. And after the class, the team meets again. They discuss the lesson. They look at all the evidence and the feedback they've collected. And they will plan the same lesson for the second time. And then one of the other teachers of the team will do it in a different class.

As you can see, it's a collaborative approach to lesson planning and lesson evaluation, which is valuable for teacher's professional development. And again, it is social. Teachers are working together and learning together. And it's situated,

实际上就相当于集体备课，教师们研究课程目标、资源和课堂活动，这是集体规划的过程。之后一名教师上课，而其他人也会去听课。一名教师在讲台上讲课，其他教师认真观察，记录课堂情况。听课的教师重点关注的是学生。他们重点关注学生在做什么。下课之后，这个小组的教师再一次进行讨论，分析收集到的情况以及反馈。随后再进行第二次备课，重新规划。然后就轮到另外一名教师，给另外一个班上课，如此循环往复。

大家可以看到，这实际上是一个集体的课程规划和评估活动，这对教师的职业发展非常重要。而且，这是具有社交性的，教师能够彼此进行交流和学习；此外，它有具体的情境，都是发生在学校和教室里的，而不是纯理论的。这种活动能不断延续，可以一直做下去。同一堂课可以进行反复改动，然后再进行下一堂课，因此这是一个循环。教师可以控制整个过程，自行决定课堂重点和评估方法，没有其他人指手画脚。也许一开始教师会获得一些外部指导，但这最终都是由教师自己来规划的。

同辈观察

我再简单说说同辈观察。我每次到中国都经常会问："你们做过同辈观察吗？"许多教师都说做过。许多教师都会说："我做过同辈观察。"但是我发现，他们的做法和我理解的同辈观察不太一样。所以我要先解释一下我对同辈观察的理解。

首先是"同辈"这个概念。同辈就是同事，不是上级。不是校长，也不是系主任。如果系主任来听你的课，这就不是同辈观察；如果校长来听你的课，这也不是同辈观察。因为如果是校长来听课的话，他们通常都是来对你进行评估的。我们说的不是这个。我们说的同辈观察，是由同事进行观察的，所以首先你需要一个你信任的同事。

你需要找一个信任的人，因为你要请他到教室里，在上完课之后和他进行讨论。你肯定不希望请了一个同事过来听课，然后他跑去跟所有人说在课上发生了什么。所以你必须确保这个人能够保密。

上课之前，你们需要简单聊一下，在听课之前进行简单沟通非常重要。你要跟这名教师大概说一下课程内容。而且很重要的一点是，你需要告诉听课的同事，你想让他们关注什么。教师有责任向听课的同事说明关注点，比如是关注用 PPT 或者黑板的方式，还是提问题的质量。你要提前跟听课的

because it is situated in schools and classrooms. It's not a theoretical exercise. It's a situated activity. It's extended too and the same lesson can be revisited for a number of times, and then the teachers move on to another lesson. Teachers are in control of the process. Teachers decide which lesson to focus on and decide how to evaluate it. You don't see an external trainer here telling teachers what to do. Maybe at the beginning, they can get some external support if lesson plan is a new idea for them. But it is clearly a teacher-led approach to professional development.

Peer observation

I'll just say a few words for one more, peer observation. Very often I ask teachers when I come to China, "Have you ever done peer observation?" And a lot of teachers say "Yes". Very often teachers tell me, "Yes, we've done peer observation." But when I ask them to explain to me what they've done, I realise it's not quite peer observation in the way I understand it. So let me explain what peer observation is for me.

First we have the word "peer". A peer is a colleague. It's not a superior person. It's not your principal or the head of your department. So if your head of department comes to observe you, that's not peer observation. If your principal comes to observe you, that's not peer observation. If your principal comes to observe you, they are normally coming to assess you. That's not what we are talking about. We are talking about peer observation. Peer observation is done by peers and peers are colleagues. So the first thing you need is a colleague, a colleague you trust.

It has to be someone you trust, because they are going to come to your classroom and you want to talk about your lesson afterwards. You want someone you trust because you want the observation and the discussion to be confidential (that is, you don't want the observer to tell everyone else what they saw).

Before the lesson it's important to have a chat, pre-observation meeting. You tell the observer about the lesson, what you are going to teach. And importantly, you also tell them what you would like them to focus on when they observe you. It's the teacher's job to tell the observer "could you please pay attention to the way I use PowerPoint or the way I use the blackboard or the kinds of questions I ask". It's important for the teacher to define the focus. Then you'll have the observation. Your observer will sit in the back and make some notes. And after the lesson, you sit down again and you discuss the lesson.

The purpose of peer observation is not to evaluate the teacher. It's not evaluation or assessment. It's a friendly observation. "Friendly" is an important word. The idea is to support the development of the teacher in a friendly way. That's why we don't involve the head teacher or the head of the department, because their observation is more formal.

同事说好，这样听课的同事会坐在后面做些笔记，上完课之后你们再讨论一下课堂情况。

同辈观察的目的不是评价或者评估，而是友好的观察。"友好"非常重要，是以一种非常友善的方式支持一名教师的职业发展。这就是为什么我们不涉及校长或者系主任，因为他们的观察更加正式。

这是职业发展社会化的体现，教师在一定情景下相互合作。这是在学校开展的，你不用去参加特定的课程，在学校就可以进行。而且这是持续性的。你可以定期进行同辈观察。我觉得一个月一次比较合理。它具有我们刚刚提到的优点，也就是社会化、情景化、可持续性。这是另外一种让教师具有掌控力、以教师为主导的模式。

我们还有其他的例子，如果你感兴趣可以自行阅读。辅导小组、反思小组、批判的朋友等都是一样的，都是教师在学校进行合作的不同方式。下面我详细讲一讲教师研究。

教师研究

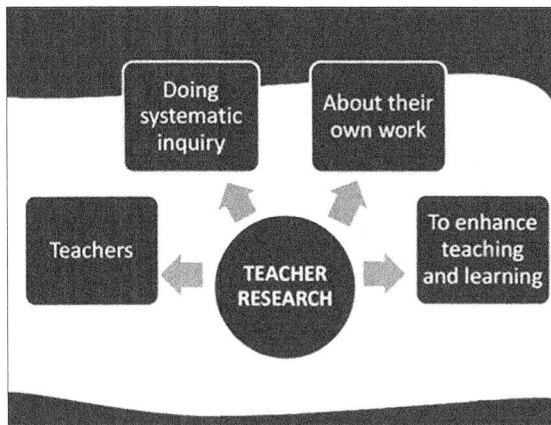

如图，教师研究有几个关键成分。我们将按照顺序逐个讨论。

教师

首先，教师研究是教师做的事情，因此它叫作教师研究。这种研究不是关于教师的研究。比如说我作为研究人员来到你的学校，问你能不能帮我填

Again this approach to professional development is social, because you have teachers working together. It's situated because it takes place in schools and classrooms. You don't have to go to a course for your peer observation. You can do it at school. It's on-going. You can do peer observation regularly. Once a month sounds reasonable to me. Social, situated, on-going, all these things we've been talking about. It's another professional development option which teachers are in control of. Also, it's teacher-led.

It's same for the other examples in the diagram above, you can read more about these if you want to. Mentoring, reflection groups, critical friends, they are all based on the sample principles of teachers working together in schools in different ways. Now the one I want to focus on in more detail is teacher research.

Teacher Research

The key components of teacher research are shown in the diagram. I will comment on each of them in turn.

Teachers

First of all, teacher research is something that teachers do. That's why it's teacher research. It's not research that is done to teachers. For example, if I come to your school as a researcher and I say, "Will you fill in this questionnaire for me?", that's not teacher research. That's research about teachers where the teachers are the participants or subjects. But in teacher research the teacher is the agent. So the first thing I want you to remember is that teacher research is something that you do. You are the agent, not (just) the object. You do it, you do not (just) receive it.

Doing systematic inquiry

Like any kind of research, teacher research involves systematic inquiry. "Systematic" means there is a system, a procedure or steps. There is an organised process. And "inquiry" means investigation. So far, then, teacher research is something that teachers do, and they do it by studying something systematically.

About their own work

What do they study? In teacher research, teachers study their own work. You study yourself. So it's something you do about yourself. It's looking inwards. It's a reflective activity. In this sense, while teachers are the agents in teacher research, they are also the focus because they study their own work.

To enhance teaching and learning

Why do we do teacher research? As for any professional development activity, the purpose of teacher research is to improve teaching and learning. The primary

写一下问卷，这不是教师研究，而是关于教师的研究，教师是参与者或被试。所以，我首先要强调的是，教师研究是你们做的研究，你们是施动者。你们做研究，而不是被研究。

系统性探究

教师研究也像其他的研究一样，涉及系统性探究。"系统性"指的是有一个内在的系统，有流程，有步骤。它有自己的流程。"探究"的意思是进行调查，因此教师研究是教师做的事情，是系统性的研究。

研究个人工作

教师研究什么呢？在教师研究中，你研究自己的工作，研究你自己，也就是你做的事情，这是内省式的研究、反思式的研究。从这个意义上讲，教师在教师研究中作为施动者的同时，他们也是焦点，因为他们研究自己的工作。

提升教学和学习效果

我们为什么要做教师研究呢？像其他的职业发展一样，我们的目的是提升教学和学习的效果。教师研究的基本目标是局部性的，即更好地理解你自己的工作（包括你的学生），并且应用这个理解取得更好的教学效果。

因此，理解教师研究这一概念非常重要。明天上午我们会概括地讲讲研究，但是今天我们只讲教师研究。教师研究是一种职业发展的手段，是对自己工作的系统性研究。这样你们才能成为更好的教师。虽然它含有"研究"这个词，但是它的实践性很强。我们谈到"研究"这个词的时候，教师一般都认为这是理论性的，只有学者才会进行研究。但是教师研究是一种实践活动，也是一种社会化活动，需要教师通过合作来完成。

我们来考虑几个情景。假设你现在是一个博士生，想要从教师那里收集一些数据。你会到不同的学校观察教师，这是你研究的一部分。这是教师研究吗？是我所定义的教师研究吗？不是。因为研究者不是在研究自己，而是在研究别人。这一点很重要，我希望你们记住。教师研究是指研究我们自己，而不是研究别人。如果你是攻读社会学位的研究生，你要请你的教师们来填写问卷。你本身也是教师，但是你让别的教师来填写问卷，这不是在研究你自己，而是在研究其他教师。请记住一点，教师研究的意思是研究我们自己（或者自己工作的某一方面，如我们的学生）。大家可能听说过行动研究，行

purposes of teacher research are local – developing a better understanding of your own work (including your students) and using that understanding to teach more effectively.

So it's very important to understand this definition of teacher research. Tomorrow morning we will talk about research more generally. But today we are talking specifically about teacher research as an approach to professional development. That's something you do. It involves systematic and careful study of your own work so that you can become a better teacher. It is practical even though the word "research" is there. I know very often when teachers see the word "research", they say "research is theoretical, research is for academics only". But teacher research is a practical activity. Teacher research can also be a social activity, when teachers do it collaboratively.

Now let's consider a few situations. Let's say you are a PhD student and you want to collect some data from teachers. You go around schools and you observe teachers as a part of your study. Is that teacher research as I defined here? Yes or no? It's not, because the person who is doing the research is not studying themselves. They are studying others. I want you to remember that. Teacher research means we are studying ourselves, not studying someone else. If you are an MA student, you are doing a Master's degree, and you go to your colleague English teachers, and you say, "Will you fill out this questionnaire for me?" You are a teacher and you are doing a research, but you are studying others. You are not studying yourself. So that's not teacher research either. It's very important to be clear about this. So teacher research means we are studying ourselves (or some aspect of our work, such as our learners). You've probably heard of action research. It's the same idea. When we do action research, who do we study? We study our own work. We study our teaching. We study our students. We don't study other people. If you are studying someone else, it is not action research. This is really important. We are talking about teacher research for professional development. It means you are studying yourself, looking in the mirror in a way, looking inwards, not outwards.

Research can be studying others. Most research involves studying others. I've done a lot of research in my career. Most of it involves studying others, studying other teachers. But what we are talking about here is studying ourselves. That's one way in which teacher research is different to conventional research. In conventional academic research, you study others. But in teacher research, we study ourselves. It's more personal.

Teacher research comes in different flavours, like ice cream. I've already mentioned action research. Self-study is another term we will come across. Self-study

动研究是教师研究的一种，概念相同。如果我们做行动研究的话，我们研究谁呢？我们研究自己的工作，研究自己的教学，研究自己的学生。我们不研究其他人。如果你研究其他人，就不叫行动研究。这一点很重要。我们说的是职业发展过程中的教师研究。它是指研究你们自己，透过镜子来向内反思自我，而不是向外研究别人。

研究也可以研究他人，而且大多数的研究都是研究他人。我也做过很多研究，大部分都是研究其他人，特别是其他教师的。但是我们这里讲的是研究自己，这是教师研究不同于传统研究的地方。传统的学术研究通常是研究他人，但是教师研究是研究我们自身的，所以这是更加私人的活动。

教师研究像冰激凌一样有不同的口味。比如，我们有行动研究，有自我研究。接下来我们也会讲到自我研究。自我研究的意思就是研究自己。探索式的研究是一个较新的术语。一些反思式研究也较新。它们有相同的核心原则，即研究我们自身，而不是别人。

教师研究的过程

在过程方面，教师研究通常是一个循环，如图。教师研究过程的版本会有所不同，每个阶段的标签也会不同，但是我们这里展示的是一个通常的版本：提问、开展教学、评估和应用。我们将依次讨论。

提问

第一步很简单，我们要提问题，提出需要找到答案的问题。这些问题是关于我们自身教学的。再强调一遍，教师研究是关于自己的研究。所以我们提出的问题必须是关于我们自己的。比如说，我的学生怎么看待这类活动，或者是这类活动的效果怎么样，又或者是如果我用这种方式来做这个活动的话，效果怎么样，会发生什么。这是我们关于自身教学的问题。因此我们必要要有问题，如果没有问题就无法进行研究。我们也可以问，学生为什么不喜欢做这种活动呢？或者，为什么我用这种方式总是没作用呢？这些都是关于教学研究的问题，这些问题来源于自身经历，所以你必须要思考你的教学方式。比如说，你希望更加深入地了解教学中的哪些环节，你对哪些问题感到困惑，又对哪些感兴趣。这样一来，你就能提出问题了。再或者，你读了一本书，或者一篇文章，你会想，这在我的课堂上是否可行？

is when you study yourself. Exploratory practice is a more recent term you might come across. And some kinds of reflective practice. They all have the same core principles, which involve studying our own work, not studying others.

The Teacher Research Process

In terms of the process, teacher research often follows a cycle, as shown below. Different versions exist, and the labels given to each stage can vary too, but the ones shown here are common: ask, do, evaluate and apply. I will comment on each of these in turn.

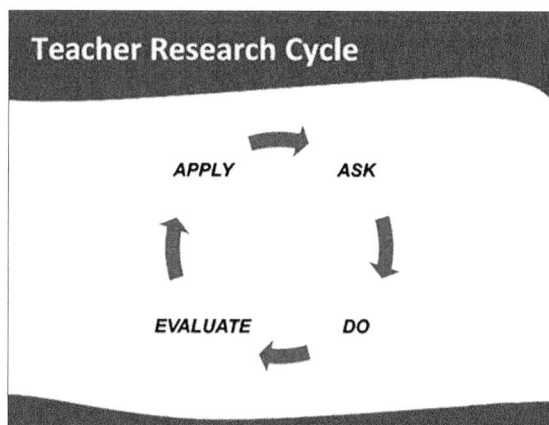

Teacher Research Cycle

APPLY   ASK

EVALUATE   DO

Ask

The first step is a simple one. We need to ask some questions. We need to ask questions that we want answers to. These questions will be questions about our own teaching. Again, teacher research is about ourselves. So the questions we ask must be about ourselves. It could be "How do my learners feel about this kind of activity?" or "How effective is this kind of activity." or "I wonder what would happen if I change the way I use activity and do it this way." They have to be questions about our teaching that we want to answer. That's always the starting point, questions. If you don't have any questions, you can't start. Another question would be "Why is it that learners don't seem to enjoy this kind of activity?" or "Why is it when I do this activity this way it never seems to work?" These are all questions about our teaching. And these questions will come from your experience of course. So you need to think about your teaching. You say, "What is there in my teaching

这也是一个问题。

开展教学

一旦你有了一些问题，你就需要采取行动来解决他们。例如，为了回答问题，你首先要做的是开展教学活动，在课堂上尝试一些教学方法，比如说新的听力教学方式、新的语法教学方式或者新的词汇教学方式。你的问题就是这种教学方式效果如何，学生是否会接受。在活动结束后，你可以把发生的事情记录下来，或者收集一些学生的反馈或作业。或者你可以录像。我们要收集依据，这就是系统性的探究，以论据为基础，而不是全凭印象来判断。不能仅仅基于"这个看起来行得通，我觉得这堂课讲得不错"这样的言论就进行评估。我们应该进一步探究，如何证明这门课上得不错。

评估

第三步是评估，评估你收集到的信息。这就是通常所称的数据分析和广义的研究解读。通过分析你收集到的信息，例如学生反馈、录像、学生作业等，你可以得到一些答案，这些答案可以解答你在过程的开始阶段提出的问题。

应用

最后，我们怎样应用我们从分析中学到的东西呢？我们需要把它应用到下一个教学环节中。你可能尝试了一种新的教学活动，但效果并不理想。你得到了一些建议，知道了为什么收效甚微。可能是你的指示不够明确，或者没有给学生足够的时间，也可能是没有让学生做好充分的准备。那么下一次就要给学生更多的时间，或者让你的指示更加清晰。然后再次尝试一下这个环节，看看效果怎么样。

这就是教师研究的过程。我给大家举一个例子，是最近我共事过的一名教师开展的教师研究项目。这名开展研究的教师叫作 Andy，他在英国一所学校从事英语外语教学工作。这个学校的管理层决定引入一种在线学习平台，也就是一个网站，供学生使用。这个学校希望大部分作业都能在平台上完成，他们要将传统的用纸笔完成作业的方式转变为线上完成的方式。学生要登录网站，在网站上完成作业，这就是这个学校要进行的改革。Andy 不确定这种方式能否受到学生的欢迎。因此他有这样一个问题：我的学生对于传统和在线完成作业的方式分别是什么样的态度？所以他想了解

that I want to understand better? What is it about my teaching that puzzles me or troubles me or interests me?" That's where your questions come from. Or maybe you read something in a book or an article, and you might say, "I wonder if that would work in my classroom." That's a question as well.

Do

Once you have some questions you need to take some action in order to answer them. For example, in response to your questions you might try out something practical in the classroom. Maybe a new way of listening, a new type of grammar activity, a new type of vocabulary activity. And your question might be "I wonder how this works. I wonder if learners will like it". After the activity you might write down a description of what happened or collect some feedback from the students or collect the work they produced. Or maybe your video recorded yourself doing the lesson. Systematic inquiry is based on evidence, not just on impressions, not just on "Oh yeah that seems to go well; that seems to be a good lesson". Teacher research goes further than that. Where is the evidence that it was a good lesson? That's what we are looking for.

Evaluate

The third stage of the process is to evaluate the information you have collected. This is what is normally called data analysis and interpretation in research more generally. By analysing the information you have – student feedback, video recordings, student work, etc. – you can formulate some answers to the questions you asked at the start of the process.

Apply

Finally, what do we do with what we learn from the analysis? We take it forward. We apply it to the next cycle of teaching. So maybe I've tried that new activity and it didn't really work. I got some evidence that helped me understand why it didn't work. Maybe my instructions weren't clear. Maybe I didn't allow it enough time. Maybe I didn't give the students enough preparation. I understand it now. So for the next cycle I'm going to give them more time. I'm going to make my instructions a bit clearer. And I'm going to try again.

This is the process of teacher research. Let me illustrate this with a real example from a teacher I worked with. One teacher I worked with recently, his name was Andy. He teaches English as a foreign language in the UK. In his school the management had decided that they wanted to introduce an online learning platform, a platform for learning which the students will use. The school wanted most of their homework to be set on the platform. So they were moving from traditional homework, you know, with pencils, pens, paper, to online homework.

他的学生对于完成作业的不同方式的态度，因为他不确定学生是否喜欢这样的改革。

在线完成作业的这种方式也非常常见，因为现在有越来越多的学校和教育机构都在使用线上教学系统，他们通常认为这种教学方式更好，或者说学生会更喜欢这种方式。但是 Andy 对此不太确定，因此他决定要对此进行研究。

他所做的是，在大约 12 周的时间里，给自己的学生留不同类型的作业。有的时候给他们布置传统的作业，比如必须要用纸笔完成的语法练习或者传统的写作练习。有的时候则是需要在网上完成的作业，学生必须要登录系统，完成网上的练习。每周他都给学生布置不同类型的作业。每次留作业之后他都会让学生填一个很短的问卷，了解一下学生在做作业时候的感受，是否觉得这份作业有用。他希望借此来了解他们对不同类型作业的态度。这项研究进行了大约 12 周，他还与一些学生进行了访谈，询问学生对于不同类型作业的感受如何。

之后，他根据所收到的信息反馈得出了一个结论：大部分学生其实并不愿意在网上完成作业，而是更愿意用传统的方式来完成作业，也就是学生拿到一张卷子，然后完成上面的练习。当然，原因不尽相同。有一些是技术上的原因，比如学生登录不进去，或者是 Wi-Fi 连接有问题。但有些学生表示，他们更喜欢手里有书有纸的感觉，更愿意拿笔去写，这样给他们的感觉会更实在。

能够更深入地了解学生的想法是十分有趣的。当然，这项研究的结果就是，他进一步确定了自己要继续用混合的方式给学生留作业。他会留一些线上作业，因为这是学校要求的，但同时他也会继续用传统的方式给学生留作业。这就是一个简单且系统的教师研究的范例。这项研究让他更深入地了解了自己的学生，而且在实际教学中他也可以运用这些结论，使教学对学生更有帮助。

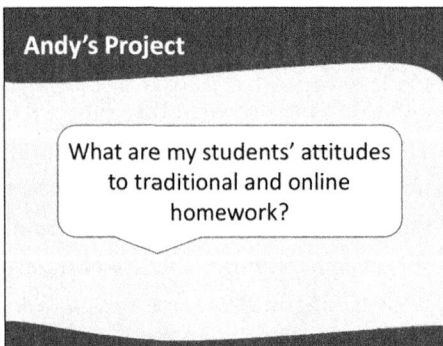

The students would log onto the website and do the exercises online. That was the move that the school was making. Andy wasn't quite sure about that. He wasn't sure whether the students would respond well. So he had a question. His question was "What are my students' attitudes to traditional and online homework?" He wanted to learn more about how his students felt about different types of homework because he wasn't sure whether they would be happy about the move to online homework.

This is quite a common situation, because today more and more schools and universities and institutions are using online systems for teaching. And the assumption very often is that these are better or that the students will like them more. But Andy wasn't sure and he wanted to investigate.

So over about 12 weeks, he gave his students different types of homework. Sometimes he gave them traditional homework. Grammar exercises that they had to do them with pens and paper or traditional writing exercises. And sometimes he gave them online homework, using the new platform. They had to log onto the system and complete the exercises online. So every week he gave the students different types of homework. And after each homework, he asked them to fill in a short questionnaire where they gave their opinions about whether they enjoyed doing the homework or if they thought it was useful. He was trying to understand how they felt about the different types of homework. And they did this for, I said about 12 weeks. And he interviewed some of his students as well and asked them about different approaches to homework and how they felt about.

And then he looked at all this evidence and he was able to arrive at some conclusions. And the conclusion he reached was that most of his students did not prefer the online homework. This was his discovery that most of his students preferred to continue doing homework in a more traditional way, in other words, to be given an exercise on a piece of paper and to write it down. And there were various reasons. Some of the reasons were technical. They had problems logging onto the website. They had problems with Wi-Fi connections. But some of them said, "We just like the feel of the piece of paper or the book in our hands. We like the feel of the pen while we are writing. It's a lot more tactile, concrete."

It was very interesting for him to have this deeper understanding of his students. Of course, as a result of his study, he continued to give the students a mixture of homework. He gave them some online homework, because that was the requirement from the school. But he also made sure he continued to give them some more traditional homework as well. This is a simple but systematic example of a teacher doing teacher research. As a result of that, he developed a better understanding of his students. And he obtained information that he could use in his teaching in order to

从这个例子可以看出，教师研究是由教师开展的、关注自身和学生的研究。这个研究非常系统。他有计划，有研究问题，有数据，有调查问卷，有实用目的，也有数据分析。他还将研究结果运用到了未来教学策略的制订上。

教师研究的益处

有很多文献都讲到了教师研究对教师的益处，我给大家总结了几点。

自信

教师经常说，在进行教师研究后，他们更自信了，对自己的职业更自信了，因为他们觉得自己对教学和学习有了更好的理解。

动力

动力更强了。这也跟我之前讲的有关系，我们需要有职业发展，这样才能对自己的工作保持热情。根据教师们自己的说法，通过做这样的教师研究项目，他们能够对教学以及教学学习有持续的热情。

批判意识

教师说他们对于自己工作的批判意识更强了。其实，批判意识并不是消极的含义，而是说教师开始对自己的行为提出问题。他们不会做出各种理所当然的假设，说我知道我的学生喜欢在线的作业方式，而是去进行研究得出结论。所以不再做假设，而是提出问题，这就是批判精神的意义。

了解

在进行教师研究之后，教师对于自己的教学和学生也有了更深的了解。

自主性

教师更具有自主性了。这是因为他们是在自己的教室里面开展研究，通常没有来自外界的支持。并且，我们所说的自主性是和之前提到的"机器人"相对立的。教师研究可以帮助教师拥有良好的自我感觉。

毫无疑问，教师研究对于教师来说是有很多益处的。和我一起共事过的一名教师说："你会觉得进行了行动研究会为你带来改变；这个研究并不是纯粹为了个人目的，而是着眼于实际运用。"所以这是教师研究非常重要的一个目的，它并不完全是为了得出一些理论，而是为了能够让教师实实在在地从中受益。另外一位教师提到了自己做教师研究的经验。她说："我要推荐它，

make his teaching more useful and more beneficial for the students.

So as we can see from this example, teacher research is something that teachers do. It's something where teachers focus on themselves and their students. And it is quite a systematic process. He had a plan. He had questions. He collected some evidence. He used questionnaires and interviews and he analysed the information he collected. He also used what he learned to make decisions about future teaching.

Benefits of Teacher Research

Much has been written about the benefits of teacher research. Here are some ways in which it can help teachers.

Confidence

Teachers often say that as a result of doing teacher research, they feel more confident, more professionally confident in their work, because they have a better understanding of teaching and learning.

Motivation

Teachers also say they feel motivated by teacher research. And this goes back to the point I made earlier that we need professional development so that we remain excited about our work. Teachers say that "As a result of doing a project, I'm now very motivated to continue teaching and learning about teaching".

Criticality

Teachers say they become more critical about their work. Critical not in the sense of negative, but critical in the sense of they question everything they do. They don't make assumptions any more. They don't say "I know my learners like online homework". They don't say that. They find out. They investigate. Not making assumptions but asking questions. That's part of being critical.

Understanding

Teachers say that after doing teacher research they have a better understanding of their teaching and of their students.

Autonomy

And teachers also say that they feel more autonomous. They feel a greater sense of autonomy, because they've done this project in their classroom, very often without much support. And being autonomous is the opposite of being a robot (we discussed different metaphors for teachers earlier). So teacher research can help teachers feel better about themselves.

There is no doubt that teacher research has many benefits for teachers. One teacher I worked with recently said that "You can feel you are making a difference with action research; it is not about researching purely for personal gain, but is

Benefits

IMPACT of TR

- Confidence
- Motivation
- Criticality
- Understanding
- Autonomy

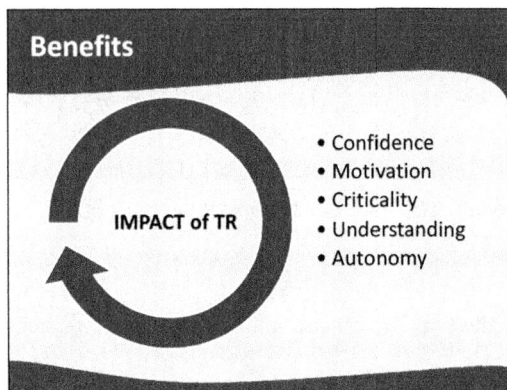

因为教师研究改变了我对于课堂上教学体验的理解，也改变了我对于自己教学的理解。"这种改变是指对自己的课堂行为及其原因提出质疑。这是件好事，因为很多时候教师工作了很多年之后就有了一套模式，不再对自己的教学提出质疑，也不会再去想我为什么这么教这样的问题了。我们只是在做。所以如果能够通过质疑自己来打破这种套路，这将对我们的职业发展有所增益。这样做是有益处的，在职业的意义上讲是有益处的。

教师研究的批评

当然，也有一些对于教师研究的批评意见，有一些人就批评了教师研究。Dörnyei（2007，p.191）在几年前对行动研究提出过这样的意见。他说迄今为止做行动研究的教师还非常少，他还没有遇到过一个自己有意愿要进行这种行动研究项目的教师，都是被迫去做的。我不确定他的批评在当时是否有效，但它们现在肯定是无效的。现在世界各地都有教师自愿参加的教师研究项目。有一些由诸如剑桥大学出版社或英国文化委员会这样的机构主导。所以我认为这样评价教师研究是不真实的，因为还是有教师在做教师研究的，而且是自愿的。

还有另外一种最近由 John Hattie 提出来的批评意见。他是一名非常知名的学术研究学者。但是他对于教师研究提出了这样的意见，他说："研究是一项具体的技能……我们中有一些人花了很多年才学会这项技能。让教师去做研究者？他们并不是研究者。"我觉得这种观点很令人失望，因为他非常消极。他并不认为教师能够在自己的课堂里面做研究。我完全不同意这种观点。他的观点很有意思，因为他其实没有按照我所说的教师研究的概念去想这个问题。我认为教师研究是基于课堂的实际研究，而他说的这个完全是纯学术的研究。所以，他的这个观点完全是基于他对于教师研

focused on practical application". So teacher research has a concrete impact. It's not a theoretical activity but research that teachers do for very concrete, practical benefits. Another teacher talked about her experience of teacher research as follows: "I would recommend it as it has certainly shaken up my view of how I learn from my experiences in the classroom and what I base my understandings of my teaching on." So in this case teacher research made the question what they are doing in the classroom and why. It is a good thing to be shaken up a little bit because sometimes, when we've been teaching for many years, we get into a routine, and we stop asking questions about what we do and why we do it. We just do it. So it's good if we give ourselves a little shake and disturb the comfortable routine by asking challenging questions. It's healthy to do that, healthy in a professional sense.

Criticisms of Teacher Research

Of course there have also been criticisms of teacher research. Some people have criticised teacher research. Several years ago, Dörnyei (2007, p.191) wrote this about action research: "There is still too little of it... I am still to meet teacher who has been voluntarily involved in an action research project." I am not sure his criticisms were valid back then, but they certainly are not now. Today there are several teacher research schemes around the world which teachers participate in willingly. Some of these schemes are supported by leading organisations such as Cambridge University Press or The British Council. So I do not think it is true to criticise teacher research because very few teachers do it or do it willingly.

Another criticism I came across recently was this one by John Hattie, a very well-known academic. When asked about teachers being researchers, he said, "Researching is a particular skill... Some of us took years to gain that skill. Asking teachers to be researchers? They are not." I find this quite disappointing because he is being quite dismissive, quite negative about whether teachers can actually do research in their own classrooms. I disagree completely with this. It's interesting to think about his position, because I think he is not thinking about teacher research as I defined it, as a practical classroom-based activity. He is thinking research as an academic activity. That's what he was talking about. So I think these comments are based on a misunderstanding of what teacher research is. He said it took him many years to become a very successful academic researcher but when we promote teacher research we are not trying to make teachers professional researchers. Rather, we want them to use research to become better teachers. Teachers do research for professional development, not for academic purposes so it is a different type of activity. So the criticism above is based on a misunderstanding

究的误解。他说他花了很多年的时间才成为一名成功的学术研究者，但当我们提倡教师研究时，我们并不是让教师成为专业的研究人员，而是希望他们运用研究成为更好的教师。教师做研究是为了职业发展，而不是为了学术的目的。这里的研究种类是不一样的。所以如果有人说教师做不了研究，那通常是因为他们没有真正理解教师研究是什么。他们脑子里只有学术研究，还觉得这些研究结果通常只适用于个人，而不具备普适性。这也无妨，因为教师想用这些结果去提高他们自己的教学。此外，教师研究的价值不只体现在结果上，还体现在过程中。最近我（Borg 2016，p.4）发表了这样一个观点，我认为教师研究的好处并不在于能够产生一锤定音的结论，而是在于能够让教师在职业上重振，再次发现自己的力量，重拾自己的激情，在任何特定计划得出正式结论后的很长一段时间内都是如此。重振指你发现自己的力量，重拾自己的热情。这是教师研究的最大的好处之一。它让教师们再次振作，重拾对工作的热情。几年前我在巴基斯坦和几名教师共事，其中一人最后说："我们的教学方式从十年前就没有过任何改变。"他们说，在研究开始前，他们就用这种方式教了十年。你可以想象他们说话时疲惫的语气。"年年都一样。""但现在（体验了教师研究后）我们渴望把新方式运用到教学中。"这是很重要的一个好处。这就是职业重振。

第二个好处是"态度上的调整"，即改变你对工作的态度。做了教师研究的教师们说，他们现在对自己的工作、教学和学生有了不同的了解。教师会说："行动研究改变了我对教学和职业的态度。"这种转变会持续很长时间，即使以后他们不再做教师研究，这种态度的转变还是会长期存在。这点非常重要，教师研究所带来的不仅仅是结果，还有其他的好处。

下面我们来总结一下教师研究，主要有以下几点：

- 教师研究有完善的理论依据。
- 教师研究在世界许多国家都有开展。
- 教师可以从教师研究活动中收获许多益处。
- 也有一些批评意见，我们需要注意并且以一种合理的方式来回应。

of what teacher research is. When people say teachers can't be researchers they very often do not really understand what teacher research is. They are thinking of academic research. And they are very often thinking about the quality of the results. But the results that emerge from teacher research are normally of local value rather than being generalisable. That is OK because the teacher wants to use those results to improve their own practice. Also, in teacher research there is great value in the process too, not just the results. Recently I wrote that the benefits of teacher research are not just "in generating clear-cut results, but in providing the kinds of professional reinvigoration and attitudinal realignment that will stay with teachers long after the formal conclusion of any particular... scheme" (Borg 2016, p.4). Reinvigoration is the way you rediscover your strength, you rediscover your enthusiasm. That's one of the main benefits of teacher research. It helps teachers become reinvigorated, to discover their enthusiasm for the job again. I worked with some teachers in Pakistan a few years ago in a teacher research scheme. One of them said in the end, "We have been teaching the same way we taught ten years ago." They said "before this project, we've been teaching the way for ten years." You just have to try to imagine how they said it with this sort of tired voice. "Year after year, it was the same." "But now (after experiencing teacher research) we have an urge to experiment with new ideas in our teaching." This is a very important type of benefit. This is professional reinvigoration.

The second point is that this quotation is "attitudinal realignment", which is changing your attitude towards your work. Teachers who have done teacher research say, "Now I'm looking at my work differently. I have a different understanding of my teaching. I have a different understanding of my learners." This is what we mean by changing attitudes. And these changes "will stay with teachers long after the formal conclusion of any particular... scheme". Even if they are not doing action research or teacher research any more, changes in teachers' attitudes can be long-lasting. So this is really important. Teacher research is not just about results, but there are other benefits too.

At this point I would like to summarise what I have said so far about teacher research. The main points are:

- There are good theoretical reasons for teacher research.
- Teacher research is happening in many countries around the world.
- Teachers can experience a whole range of benefits through teacher research.
- There are also some criticisms, which we need to be aware of and be able to respond to in a reasonable way.

进行教师研究的建议

以下是进行教师研究的 18 条建议，但是我只推荐其中的 12 条。所以，请阅读下面的清单，判断哪 12 条是我想要推荐的建议。

第一条　把教师研究融入日常的教学活动中。

第二条　要尽快完成教师研究项目，越快越好。

第三条　研究一个对你的同事和学校都有意义的问题。

第四条　教师研究项目越复杂越好。

第五条　把"规模小但质量高"作为你的座右铭。

第六条　寻找一些能使教师研究成为一项合作式活动的方法。

第七条　找一个"批判性朋友"来帮助你反思整个研究过程。

第八条　要记住教师研究可能会占据你额外的时间。

第九条　开始教师研究项目前先去上一门统计学的课。

第十条　一定要证明一些事情，否则这个项目就是浪费时间。

第十一条　关注与你的工作紧密相关的实际问题。

第十二条　确保你的计划在现有的资源条件下是可行的。

第十三条　找机会和同事谈谈你正在做的项目。

第十四条　一旦明确了该项目不能让你得到你所希望的结果，就应该尽快放弃。

第十五条　不要尝试去做一个研究者，开展教师研究是为了帮助你成为一个更好的教师。

第十六条　对收集和分析数据的相关知识有一个基本的了解。

第十七条　请求你的上司减少你的工作量，以便你能很好地完成这个项目。

第十八条　进行一些与研究主题相关的背景阅读。

我来给大家谈一谈这些建议，我把它们分成四组，每一组包含三条。

第一组

第一组包括第五条、第十六条和第十八条。它们都与教师研究中"质量"的概念有关。

Tips for Doing Teacher Research

Below is a list of 18 tips for doing teacher research. I would only recommend 12 of these though, so before reading on please look at the list and decide which 12 you think I would recommend.

1. Integrate teacher research into normally occurring teaching and learning activities.
2. Complete your teacher research project as quickly as possible.
3. Examine an issue that is of interest to your colleagues and school generally.
4. Make the project as complex as possible.
5. Make "small-scale but high-quality" your motto.
6. Look for ways to make teacher research a collaborative activity.
7. Find a "critical friend" who can help you think things through.
8. Remember that teacher research will make additional demands on your time.
9. Take a course in statistics before you start your teacher research project.
10. Make sure you are able to prove something – otherwise the project is a waste of time.
11. Focus on a practical issue which is of immediate relevance to your work.
12. Ensure that your plans are feasible given the resources available.
13. Look for opportunities to talk to colleagues about the work you are doing.
14. Abandon the project as soon as it becomes clear that it will not provide the results you were hoping for.
15. Don't try to become a researcher, but do teacher research to help you become a better teacher.
16. Become familiar with basic issues in collecting and analysing research data.
17. Ask your line manager for a reduction in your workload so that you can do your project.
18. Do some background reading related to your topic.

I will talk about these tips now by organising them into four groups, each with three items.

Group 1

The first group contains items 5, 16 and 18. These all related to the idea of "quality" in teacher research.

第五条是说教师研究应该是小规模的，因为这是你要在课堂中开展的研究，可能是你日常工作的一部分，所以必须是小规模的。但是同时也必须是高质量的，这点很重要。有的时候人们会认为教师研究不是什么好研究，事实上并不是这样的。我们还是要保证它的高质量。但是你可以控制它的规模，确保它是一个可行的研究。

第十六条也与质量相关，如果你要做教师研究，你不必去上有关研究数据的课程，但是你必须要对收集和分析数据相关的知识有一些最基本的了解。比如说你要给学生做一个简单的问卷，你必须要在设计问卷时确保其质量。所以你必须要对设计问卷有一些基本的了解。学生反馈了结果以后，你必须要分析数据，所以你也必须要有分析数据的基本能力。我开展的一些项目中通常会有一个工作坊，教给教师们一些最基本的数据分析技巧。我们不希望教师研究太技术化，但是"在收集和分析数据中必须要体现一定程度的（不一定是'科学的'）严格，这样我们才能够对教师研究所产生的结果拥有自信"（Borg 2013，p.20）。这点很重要，因为你要收集、分析数据，要得到结果，要运用这些结果来制订教学上的决策，决定如何改变自己的教学。所以你当然希望你能够信任这些研究成果，否则的话，你做出来的决定所基于的就是不可靠的研究结果。这就是为什么我们需要在教师研究中体现一定程度的严格。

第十八条，进行一些与研究主题相关的背景阅读。这是另一个提升教师研究质量的方法。你的主题可能会涉及使用某些技术，或者要进行反馈，或者是评估写作，或者是要教语法。无论你的主题是什么，进行一些与研究主题相关的背景阅读总是有帮助的。我并不是说要你读100本书或者500篇文章之类的，而是指你必须要看看有哪些文献与你的主题相关，这会对你很有帮助。因为如果你没有去了解这方面已经做了哪些研究，你很可能会重蹈覆辙。但如果你读了别人做过的研究，就可以给你些启发，并用到自己的研究上。因此做一点背景阅读是很有帮助的，但不用做太多。我知道有的时候对于教师来说，要获得这些阅读的材料其实很难，但是这些背景阅读其实很重要。

所以我把这三条都分到教师研究的"质量"这一类上。规模小更容易达到高质量。对收集和分析数据的相关知识有一个基本的了解也能够提高教师

Item 5 suggests that teacher research should be small-scale, because this is something you have to do in your classroom. This is something you will probably have to do as a part of your normal work. It has to be small-scale but high-quality. Quality matters. People sometimes say that teacher research means bad research. That's wrong; it still needs to be high-quality, but you can keep it small-scale to make it feasible.

Item 16 also relates to quality. If you want to do teacher research you do not have to do a research methods course first. But you do need to have some basic understanding of issues related to collecting data and analysing data. For example, if you want to give your students a simple survey, a simple questionnaire, you need to design it, and you need to design it in a way that it's good quality. So you need to have some basic understanding of how to do this. And when you get the results back from your students, you need to analyse those results. So you need to have some basic understanding of what to do there too. On some of the projects that I work on we run workshops for teachers where we give them some basic ideas about data collection and analysis that they can use. We do not want to make teacher research too technical, but "a basic level of (not necessarily 'scientific') rigour must apply to the collection and analysis of data if teacher research is to generate findings we can have confidence in" (Borg 2013, p.20). This is important because you are going to collect and analyse data and then you are going to use the results to make decisions about teaching. You might use those results to decide maybe how to change your teaching. So you want those results to be results you can trust. Otherwise, you will make decisions based on unreliable results. That's why it's important that we have a basic level of rigour in doing teacher research.

The third item in this first group (18) is about doing some background reading. This is another way to improve the quality of teacher research. So maybe your topic is using some kind of technology or doing feedback or assessing writing or teaching grammar. Whatever the topic is, it is useful to do a little bit of background reading. Again, it doesn't mean you have to read 100 books or 500 articles. Of course not. But it does mean having a look to see whether there is anything that has been written about your topic that could help you. Because if we don't know what's already there, we might simply be reinventing the wheel (repeating what others have already done). And if we read what other people have done, that can give us good ideas we can use in our project. So it's useful to do a little bit of background reading, not a lot. I know it's sometimes difficult for teachers to get access to materials to read, but generally it is a good idea to do some background reading.

So in this first group we have three items that relate to the quality of teacher research. Keeping projects small makes it easier to achieve high-quality. Having

研究的质量。此外，做背景阅读也可以提高质量。

第二组

第二组是第一条、第八条和第十二条，这些是和"可行性"相关的。这一点很重要，因为如果项目不可行的话，我们就不能完成。

第一条说的是要把教师研究融入日常的教学活动当中去。这是一个很好的建议。我们希望教师能够把研究和自己的日常工作融合到一起，这也会让你做研究时更轻松一些，而不是说让你做一个完全和工作无关的，或者完全改变你日常工作的研究。比如说你是教阅读的，你就可以把关于阅读的教师研究和课程结合在一起，这样会让研究做起来更容易，也更可行。

第八条提醒我们，教师研究总是会占据你额外的时间。它意味着无论你将研究和你自己的日常工作结合得多紧密，你都要拿出额外的时间去做研究。比如说你不得不设计学生的问卷，要去分析结果，等等。所以我们要尽量把教师研究整合到日常工作中，但是永远要记得它还是会额外占用你的时间的。

还有第十二条，确保你的计划在现有的资源条件下是可行的。这一点非常重要。你要对自己的资源和计划进行评估，确保两者能相匹配。资源是什么呢？首先是时间，这是最重要的资源。你有没有额外的时间可以用于教师研究项目？如果你没有时间去进行职业发展，那么也就做不了教师研究。所以，如果没有时间，你启动这样的研究项目也就没有任何意义了。这点十分重要。有的教师一周教 40 节课，对于这样的教师我就不建议他们做教师研究了，因为他们没有时间。我会给他们寻找其他进行职业发展的方法。尽管我们不需要额外花费很多时间去做教师研究，但还是需要花上一些时间的。时间是最重要的一个资源，当然还需要其他的资源，比如设备。所以在考虑进行教师研究的时候，你要想想自己手头有哪些资源。可能你上半年很忙，下半年很闲，那么你就可以在下半年做教师研究。切合实际十分重要。

所以这三条建议都与可行性有关。如果我们可以确保教师研究计划更加可行，我们就更可能高质量完成。

some understanding of collecting and analysing data also improves the quality of teacher research. And background reading can also contribute to the quality of teacher research.

Group 2

In the second group of suggestions I've got items 1, 8 and 12. They are related to the idea of "feasibility", which is very important because if a project is not feasible then it may not be completed.

Item 1 says it's a good idea to "Integrate teacher research into normally occurring teaching and learning activities". That's really a good piece of advice. We are trying to integrate teacher research into what we normally do. The idea is that you can integrate your teacher research into what you normally do without having to make big changes to your normal routines. You normally teach reading lessons, and you can integrate a teacher research project about reading into that, for example. That makes it easier for you to do, and it makes it more feasible.

The second item in this group (8) reminds us, though, that teacher research will always make additional demands on your time. There will always be a little bit of extra work for teacher research, no matter how well you integrate it into what you normally do. It's always going to be a little bit of extra work. If you want to give your students a questionnaire, you have to design it. It's a little bit of extra work there. You have to analyse the results, a little bit of extra work there. So the idea is to integrate teacher research into what you normally do but we mustn't forget there will always be a little bit of extra work.

Item 12 says "Ensure that your plans are feasible given the resources available". This is really important. You should assess your research plan and assess your resources, and make sure the two match. By resources what do I mean? I mean time. It's the most obvious resource. Do you have any extra time that you can dedicate to your teacher research project? If you have zero time available for professional development, you can't do teacher research. There is no point in starting if you haven't got the time. It's really important. I know some teachers who teach 40 lessons a week. With those teachers, I don't recommend teacher research. They haven't got any time. We find other approaches to professional development that they can do. So it's not that we need many hours of extra time to do teacher research, but you do need some time. So that's the most obvious resource. There are other resources that you may need too, such as equipment. So make sure that when you are thinking about doing teacher research, you think about the resources available. Maybe you are very busy in the first part of the year, but less busy in the second part of the year. Then it will make sense to do teacher research in the

第三组

第三组包含第三条、第十一条和第十五条，它们是和"相关性"有关的。

我们先来看第十一条，关注与你的工作紧密相关的实际问题，因为这条非常明显。教师在选择研究的项目时，应该选择实际的问题，与自身工作直接相关的问题。这一点很重要。教师研究的主题应该切合实际，并且与正在做的工作相关。

第三条说的是，研究一个对你的同事和学校都有意义的问题。你之所以选了一个研究主题，肯定是因为这个主题对你而言具有意义，且它和自己的教学有关联。但是如果你能找到一个对你的学校和同事也有意义的主题，那么你就更有可能得到他们的支持，你的同事也更有可能对你做的项目感兴趣，也会更愿意帮助你。所以我们在选择主题的时候，不要光选择自己感兴趣而别人都不感兴趣，或者说与你的院系、学校都无关的主题，应该选择一个自己与同事都感兴趣的主题。

第十五条，在相关性方面和其他几条略有不同。这条说的是，不要尝试去做一个研究者，开展教师研究是为了帮助你成为一个更好的教师。我觉得这条和教师的职业身份有关。我想这也是非常有帮助的一条建议。你的首要职责、首要职业身份永远都是教师。这才是你做教师研究的原因。你的目的并不是想要成为研究人员。这是另外一个不同的身份。你做教师研究是因为你想要成为更好的教师，你想要增强自己主业的职业素养，而不是削弱它，去适应另一个角色。这一点很重要。因为有时候教师就跟我说："我并不适合这个研究者的身份，因为我毕竟还是一名教师。"所以由此我就可以看出来，他们是在教师和研究员这两种不同的身份之间挣扎，他们觉得这两种身份非常不同，甚至互为相反面。我想让他们明白，教师研究进一步增强了你现有的职业身份，帮助你成为更好的教师。因为我们在这里说的不是学术研究，而是说用于职业发展的教师研究。所以，我们认为教师研究可以进一步增强你的教师身份，而不是削弱这种身份。

所以以上就是相关性，你应该考虑项目与你的院系、学校和同事的相关性，还有与自己教师身份的相关性。教师研究项目与这些方面相关是很重要的。

second part of the year. It's important to be practical.

So these three tips have to do with feasibility. If we can make teacher research more feasible, we are more likely to complete a good quality project.

Group 3

The next group of three tips contains statements 3, 11 and 15. The common theme is "relevance", as I explain below.

I will start with Item 11 because this is quite obvious. When teachers choose a topic for teacher research they should identify a practical issue that is of immediate relevance to their own work. That's very important. The focus of teacher research should be practical and relevant to the work they currently do.

Item 3 says "Examine an issue that is of interest to your colleagues and school generally". When we choose a topic for teacher research, we start with something that is of interest to us. So there is always personal relevance. But if you can find a topic that is also of interest to your colleagues and to your school, you're more likely to get support, because it's more likely that your colleagues will show interest in what you are doing, and then be more likely to want to help you. So it's important not to choose a topic that we are interested in but that no one else cares about or one which has no relevance to our department or our institution. It should be possible to find a topic that is of interest to us but also to those we work with.

Item 15 is a slightly different way of looking at relevance. It says "Don't try to become a researcher, but do teacher research to help you become a better teacher". The kind of relevance I am thinking about here is relevance to the teachers' professional identity. I think this is an interesting one to think about. Your primary role, your primary professional identity will always be that of a teacher. That's the reason you are doing teacher research. It's not because you want to become a researcher, which is a different role, a different identity. You are doing teacher research because you want to become a better teacher. You want to strengthen your primary role, not weaken it and adopt a different role. This is very important, because sometimes teachers say to me, "I'm not comfortable being a researcher because I'm a teacher." I can see what's going on in their mind. They are struggling with these different identities, the teacher identity and the researcher identity, which they feel very different, or even maybe opposites. What I try to help them to understand is that teacher research allows you to strengthen your identity as a professional. It helps you to be a better teacher. Because we are not talking about academic research, we are talking about teacher research for professional development and this is something that strengthens your identity as a teacher, not weakens it.

So these three tips are about relevance, relevance to your work, relevance to

第四组

我推荐的最后三条，我把他们都归到了"合作性"这一大类下面。它们是第六条、第七条和第十三条。

我们来看一下第六条，找一些能使教师研究成为一项合作式活动的方法。让教师研究成为合作式活动的方法之一就是和其他的教师一起进行团队合作。比如三个教师一起合作，你们都同意在自己的教室里做同样的项目。你们一起进行规划，一起在课堂上执行这个项目计划，然后见面一起分析。这是同一个项目，但是你们三个人分别去做。这样做有很多好处，因为可以分担责任，可以分享成功。当然如果出现困难，你们也可以共同面对，互相支持。这样的合作其实是有很多好处的。

还有第七条，找一个"批判性朋友"来帮助你反思整个研究过程。这在你独自做教师研究的时候非常有用。因为你独自一人做可能会觉得很孤单，觉得自己是孤立的。但是如果你找到一个同事或朋友，愿意听你讲述这个项目，帮你找出问题并提出意见，这就对你大有帮助。这就是我说的"批判性朋友"，他可以令你重新审视你的工作和这么做的原因，也可以给你提供不同的视角。

第十三条，找机会和同事谈谈你正在做的项目。如果你的题目使同事也感兴趣，他们就愿意听听你的项目。如果他们不感兴趣，你还说这个项目的事，他们可能很快就会逃走。此外，这不是要你和学校里的同事一直讲你的项目，不要因此打扰他们休息的时间。这不能让他们感兴趣。你要找到一个合适的机会。比如你可以在开教师会的时候，用 5 分钟的时间来跟同事聊一聊你的项目；也可以在学校网站上简要介绍一下你的项目，这样你的同事也能看到；还可以在学校或公寓的电子报上建个专栏。你可以找到更简单更合适的方式和同事分享研究想法。

以上几点就是关于合作的。增强合作是使教师研究项目更加积极的另一个有用的方法。

我们讲了这 12 条之后，还有 6 条是我不建议大家那么去做的。

第二条并不是很好的建议，即"要尽快完成教师研究项目，越快越好"。你不能快速完成这样的项目。因为它需要时间，需要慢慢展开。我之前也说过，职业发展只有不断地持续下去才会更有效、更全面。教师研究也是持续性的

your colleagues and your department or your school and relevance to your identity as a teacher. Making teacher research relevant in all these ways is important.

Group 4

The last three tips I recommend can be grouped under the heading of "collaboration". They are Items 6, 7 and 13.

Item 6 is "Look for ways to make teacher research a collaborative activity". One obvious way to make teacher research collaborative is to work in a team with other teachers. There might be three of you working together. And the three of you can do the same project in your own classrooms. You plan it together. You do it in your own classrooms. You meet to analyse everything together. It's one project, but three of you are doing it in your classrooms. And there are many benefits to that. You can share your responsibility. You can share the success. Of course, when it becomes difficult, you can share that as well, so you can support each other. There are many good reasons for doing teacher research collaboratively.

Item 7 is "Find a 'critical friend' who can help you think things through". This is particularly useful if you are doing teacher research alone. If you are doing it alone, it can be a lonely activity. You can feel quite isolated. So if you can find this colleague or friend who is willing to listen to you talking about your project, who can ask you (sometimes challenging) questions about your project, that person can be very useful. This is a critical friend. Critical because they can ask you challenging questions about what you are doing and why you are doing it, and maybe help you to think about things in different ways.

Item 13 is "Look for opportunities to talk to colleagues about the work you are doing". This is an interesting one. If you choose a topic that your colleagues are interested in as well, they will be interested in hearing about your work. If you choose a topic they are not interested in, of course you can try to talk to them about it but they may run away. Also, I'm not suggesting you chase your colleagues around the school and talk to them about your project all the time. Don't stop them during breaks by cornering them and talking to them about your project all the time. That's not the way to make them interested. You need to find the right time or opportunity. Maybe it's a staff meeting and you might ask for five minutes to talk about your work. Maybe your school has a website and you could use that to write a short description of your project so your colleagues can read about it. Maybe your school or your department has a newsletter and maybe you can have a column in that. Look for simple but appropriate ways of sharing your project with colleagues.

Increasing collaboration, then, is another useful way of making teacher research a more positive activity for teachers.

活动。所以你需要至少几周的时间来做教师研究项目。不能说："我要赶快做，一周就做完。"这样就没意义了。所以这不是一个好建议。

第四条也不是一个好建议，即"教师研究项目越复杂越好"。为什么要让项目复杂呢？有的人认为越复杂的项目越好。曾经有人跟我说："我完全不理解这个讲座，我一句话也没听懂，这个讲座肯定很好。"我不同意这一点。项目可以更简单，同时质量更高。没有必要把它变得那么复杂。

第九条，显然，教师研究不需要你上统计学课程。你可能完全不需要统计数字，如果你确实需要分析数字，那也是非常简单的。我相信大家也可以找人帮助你做这些数据分析。可能你只需要算一个平均数，所以不用上统计学课程。也可能你要用 Excel 设计一个饼图，你完全可以找到人帮你。教师研究并不意味着一定得提前上复杂的统计学课。

第十条也不是好的建议，它说"一定要证明一些事情，否则这个项目就是浪费时间"。"证明"具有一种盖棺定论的感觉，意味着找到它最终的答案。其实我们永远也不会知道最终答案，所以教师研究不是为了证明什么，而是为了更好地理解，并运用你的理解去改善教学。如果有人跟你说："你并没有证明什么东西。"你就可以回答："我也没有想要证明什么，我只想尝试去理解。""否则这研究就是浪费时间"，也不对。即使你的结果不清楚，也不能说你的项目一无是处，因为你可以从研究过程中受益。这点我们前面讨论过。研究不是在浪费时间。

第十四条也不是好建议，上面说"一旦明确了该项目不能让你得到你所希望的结果，就应该尽快放弃"。我经常向别人建议，不要给自己的研究提出预定的结果。那不是做研究的方式。你只是有问题需要研究，希望回答这个问题。所以你通过研究寻找答案，并不是你已经知道它会有某种结果，然后去证明这个结果。这是错误的研究方式。所以，大家自己不要说有什么预期，做教师研究就是要系统，就是为了回答自己的问题。

最后，第十七条不是非常糟糕。如果你的系主任或者校长愿意减少你的教学工作量，让你去做教师研究，这非常好。但我的经验是这不会发生。所以我跟教师们说："不要有什么期待，要假设你要在自己现有的工作负担下做研究。"如果你期待自己的工作量能够因此减少，不要抱有这样的期待。因为希望越大，失望越大，所以我告诉他们要避免失望。当然问问没有坏处，

So we have six items on the list that I would not recommend as tips for teacher research.

Item 2 is "Complete your teacher research project as quickly as possible". You cannot do teacher research quickly. Projects need time to unfold. That is what we said earlier about professional development. Professional development is more effective when it's on-going. Teacher research is an on-going activity. You need a few weeks at least to do a teacher research project. So you can't say, "I'm going to rush this and do it in a week, so it's finished." That's not the point. The point is not to finish it quickly. So that's not good advice.

Item 4 is also not good advice. It says "Make the project as complex as possible". Why do you want to make it complex? Some people think if it's complex, it must be good. I've heard people say to me, "I didn't understand a word of that lecture, it must be very good." I don't agree with that. Don't make it complex. You can keep it simple and still make it high-quality. There is no need to make things complex.

Looking at Item 9, there is certainly no need to take a course in statistics in order to do teacher research. You may not need any statistics at all. If you do need to do any analysis of numbers, it will be very simple. And I'm sure you can find someone who can help you with that if you need to. Maybe you need calculate an average and you don't need to go on a statistics course for that. Maybe you need to design a pie chart in Excel, and I'm sure you can find a friend to help you with that. Teacher research does not call for complex statistics.

Item 10 is also not good advice. It says "Make sure you are able to prove something – otherwise the project is a waste of time". "Prove" has got a certain conclusive feeling to it, as in finding out the answer once and for all. We will never find the final answer. So teacher research is not about proving; teacher research is about understanding and using that understanding to improve our teaching. If someone says to you "But you didn't prove anything", your answer should be "I wasn't trying to prove anything. I was trying to understand". "Otherwise the project is a waste of time." That's not true either. Even if your results are a bit unclear, there will be other benefits to you of going through the process, as we discussed earlier. It's not a waste of time.

Item 14 says "Abandon the project as soon as it becomes clear that it will not provide the results you were hoping for". I always say to researchers generally that you should not be hoping for any particular results. That's not the way to do research. We have questions we want to answer. We do the research, and we see what the answers are. It's not about hoping for a certain result. It's not "I know something already. I just want to prove it." That's the wrong way to go about it. So don't hope for anything. It's not about hoping. It's about doing the research

但是通常只能拿到否定的答案。即使同意了，也意味着你要在四天上完五天的课，在剩下的一天做研究。这并没有什么帮助。所以如果你的上司能够给你减少课时量，很好，但这是一个很大的挑战。

综上所述，我将教师研究的 12 条建议分成了四大类：质量、可行性、相关性和合作性。如果我们想要把教师研究做好，我们就需要考虑质量，这样我们才能对所学有信心；我们需要考虑可行性，这样才能实现我们的项目计划；我们需要考虑相关性，项目对我们、对我们的同事、对我们的学生以及对我们的学校才有意义；我们还需要考虑合作性，因为合作增添了研究的价值。如果我们做到了这些，我们就很可能在工作中变得更加成功。

如果我们知道教师研究是什么，而且我们最开始的设计正确，并具有严谨性、可行性、相关性和合作性，那么"教师研究就是职业化中非常务实的做法"（Borg 2013，p.217）。所以我希望大家有所收获和思考，而且能把这些理念带回你们所在的学校和同事分享。

*　　　　*　　　　*

☺ 交流互动

提问者 1：谢谢教授，我确实学到了很多。我的问题是关于教师研究的。如果是研究我们自己和我们的教学的话，如何确保我们得到了真正的答案？比如，我想了解我的学生如何看待我的教学方法或者教学策略。如果我直接问他们，或者做问卷调查，我担心他们不会给我真实的回答，尤其当我教的是学分课程，情况就更是如此。上个学期我问学生满不满意，他们说非常满意，但是

systematically and answering your questions.

Finally, we have Item 17. This is not a bad thing. If your school or head of your department are willing to reduce your teaching workload so you can do teacher research, that is wonderful. But my experience is that this never happens. So I say to teachers, "Don't expect anything. Assume you are going to have to do this within your existing workload." If you get something, good. But don't assume you will. Because teachers get hopeful and then they will get disappointed. So to avoid any disappointment. I say "Don't expect that". There is no harm in asking, but in my experience, the answer very often is "No". Or sometimes the answer is "Yes", but what that means is that to have one day a week for teacher research you have to squeeze your full workload into four days, which isn't particularly helpful. So if you can persuade your employer to give you some time for this kind of work, that is great. But it could be quite challenging to get the time.

To summarise, then, I have classified the 12 tips for teacher research under four headings: quality, feasibility, relevance and collaboration. If we want to do teacher research well, we need to think about quality, so that we have confidence in what we learn. We need to think about feasibility, so it's actually possible to do the project we plan. We need to think about relevance, so that project means something to us, to our colleagues, to our students, and to our school. And we need to think about collaboration, because collaboration adds value to it. If we can address all of those, we are much more likely to be successful in our work.

If we understand what teacher research is, we set it up in the right way, and we address the points I have just been talking about, then "teacher research is an eminently practical way of being professional" (Borg 2013, p.217). I hope there is something you can take back to your school and share with your colleagues as well.

*   *   *

☺ Interaction and Communication

Questioner 1: Thank you professor. I learned a lot from your lecture. My question is about teacher research. If it was research about ourselves and our own teaching, how can we make sure that we can get real answers? For example, if I want to ask my students' attitudes towards my teaching methods, or teaching strategies, if I ask them directly or do questionnaires, I'm afraid they won't give me

之后有的学生给校长写邮件来抱怨我的课程。请问如何避免这种情况呢?

Simon Borg:第一个就是非常好的问题。我觉得教师研究是个性化的活动,因为我们要观察自己。其中会提出带有主观性和偏见的问题。我们还会让学生提供反馈,看看他们有多诚实。这是我们面临的真实挑战。

举个例子,我希望学生给我一些关于我的教学的某些方面的反馈,我还需要思考,如果我问他们,他们会不会给我诚实、坦率的回答呢?如果我认为他们不会,我就不会问他们这样的问题。如果我不确定,我就会问问,看看他们到底会给出什么样的答案。然后我会观察这些数据和证据,分析这些数据的可信度,看它们是否言过其实。之后我需要解读数据,假如结果显示学生喜欢我,非常喜欢我的教学方式,那我必须要进行解读,他们这么说可能是因为我要给他们打分,或因为他们不想让我不开心。他们喜欢我,所以给出积极的回答。

如果你认为让学生直接给反馈没用,那么你最好思考一下他们为什么会这么做。也许他们担心他们所讲的会影响他们的成绩。所以,你需要先给学生解释为什么要做这个调查,并且告诉他们这是匿名的,不会影响他们的成绩。通常情况下学生不知道、不理解我们为什么问这些问题,因为我们没有解释。

所以,学生参与非常重要。如果你要做一个调查,学生需要知道你在做什么。你可以说:"我这次课想尝试不同的内容,或者阅读教学的不同方式,或者新的听力教学方式,我希望你们给我们反馈,这样我才知道这种方式是不是对你们有帮助。如果你们给我真实的反馈,我就能进行调整,这样才有利于你们的学习。"他们理解后,就更可能给出真实反馈。如果你不解释,他们会以为这种反馈和成绩有关,当然就会比较谨慎。

另外,你让学生做反馈时,有时可以让他们匿名提供。如果是匿名,他们可能更愿意坦诚相待。所以你必须思考这些问题:为什么他们不给我诚实的反馈?原因是什么?怎么解决这些问题?通过解释我们在做什么,或者采用其他方式。

这个问题非常好。我们确实需要思考主观性、偏见等因素,然后再开展教师研究。

the real answers, especially when it's a credit course. Last semester, I was asking my students whether they are satisfied; they said, "Yes, yes, we are very satisfied." But after that some of my students sent an email to our head teachers to complain about me. So how to make sure this won't happen again?

Simon Borg: That's a good question to start with. I think teacher research is quite a personal activity because we are looking at ourselves. And that raises questions about subjectivity, and about bias. And it also raises questions about asking the students for input and how honest they are willing to be. These are real challenges that we face.

So let's think about students. Let's say I want my students to give me some feedback on some aspects of my teaching, and I have to think about that if I ask them, are they likely to give honest, frank feedback? If I really don't think they will, then I probably won't ask them. If I'm not sure, I would ask them just to see what they would give back. Then I can look at the data, the evidence, to see how trustworthy these results are. Are they too positive? Then I need to interpret the results. Maybe the results say that the students like me or whatever very much. Then I need to interpret these results to see, well, probably they are just saying that because I'm going to give them a mark, or because they don't want to upset me. They like me. They want to be positive.

If you do not think that asking students for feedback is useful, it is good to think about why they are being too positive. Maybe they are worried that what they say will affect their grades. So you need to explain to them why you are asking for feedback and to tell them that it is anonymous and will not affect their grades. Very often students don't understand why we are asking them for feedback because we don't explain.

So I think involving students in the process is valuable. You are doing a project. Students need to know what's going on. You might say, "In this course I'm trying out different types of activities or different ways of teaching reading, a few ways of teaching listening, and I would really appreciate your feedback so that I can understand if it works, if it's useful for you. If you really tell me what you think, I could make adjustment and adapt it, and it would be more beneficial for your learning." And then they have this understanding, they are hopefully more likely to give honest feedback. But when they don't know why you are asking them, and they think this might have something to do with their grades, and of course they will be cautious.

Another thing is if we ask students for feedback, sometimes we could ask them to give it anonymously rather than writing their names down. When it's anonymous, they are more likely to be frank. So you have to think through these kinds of issues,

提问者 2：非常感谢您。您提到教师研究会重新激发教师的职业热情并带来态度上的转变。但是，昨天我读了一篇论文，上面提到，根据一组教师的研究，好教师不是培训出来的，而是天生的。他们给出一些优秀教师的特点，我简单列了个清单：随时做好准备；保持积极；对学生有很高的期待；有创造性；对学生很公正；能够展示个人魅力，而且能够培养一种归属感；具有同情心；富有幽默感；尊重学生；最后一点就是能够宽恕学生的错误。您能不能评价一下？

Simon Borg：当然了。我想问您一下这篇文章的出处。

提问者 2：我记不清楚了，可能是一篇由哈佛大学的一个研究团队做的报告。

Simon Borg：这里的问题是，好教师是天生的还是后天塑造的。这是长久以来不断被讨论的问题，很有趣。在很多研究中，我们要学生告诉我们，好教师有什么样的素质。如果我们问学生，他们通常只会提到这些个人特点，比如说教师要公正、有趣、幽默、和蔼、有创造力。这些都是学生经常会提及的特点。分析这些特点时，我们很容易得出一个结论，即好教师不需要培训，他们只需要有恰当的个人特质。

但是我不同意。具有这些特质非常重要，这是毫无疑问的。但是，你如果不了解你所教的学科，就不可能成为一个好教师。你可能是一个非常有趣的教师，让课堂很活跃，但是学生学不到什么东西，因为这名教师本身就没有充分掌握他所教授的学科。所以不论是数学教师、英语教师还是科学教师，培训都可以让教师对这门学科有深入的理解。这就是培训的一个作用。

because again, why is it that they won't give me honest feedback? What are the reasons? And then how can I address those? By explaining what we are doing, etc.

That's a good question. We do need to think about subjectivity, bias – these kinds of things when we are doing teacher research.

Questioner 2: Thank you Professor Borg. You said that teacher research motivates professional reinvigoration and attitudinal realignment. But I read this paper yesterday, which says, based on a group of teachers' research, that good teachers are not trained. Good teachers are born. They give a list of characteristics of good teachers. I briefly made a list. Be well prepared. Positive. Hold high expectations for students. Be creative. And be fair to the students. And display personal charisma and cultivate a sense of belonging. To be compassionate. Have a sense of humour. Respect the students. Tolerate mistakes. Could you try to comment on this?

Simon Borg: Sure. Could I ask about the source of this article you read?

Questioner 2: I don't remember clearly. This might be a report done by a group of researchers in Harvard.

Simon Borg: The basic argument here is, are good teachers born or made? This is a discussion which has been going on for a long time. It's interesting. There has been quite a lot of research; when we ask students to tell us about the qualities of a good teacher, they normally only mention these kinds of personal characteristics. They say that the teacher is fair; they say the teacher is funny, and has a sense of humour; the teacher is kind; the teacher is creative. These are the kinds of characteristics that students very often mention. And when we look at those characteristics, it's easy to reach the conclusion that good teachers don't need any training. They just need to have the right kind of personal characteristics.

I disagree. It is important to have those personal characteristics undoubtedly. But, you can't be an effective teacher, for example, if you don't have a good command of the subject you are teaching. It's just not possible. You might be a pleasant teacher and the students might have fun, but if the teacher does not have a sound understanding of the subject matter he or she cannot be effective. So one valuable function of training is to give teachers, whatever the subject is, mathematics, or science or English, whatever, a good command of the subject. So this is one thing we get from training.

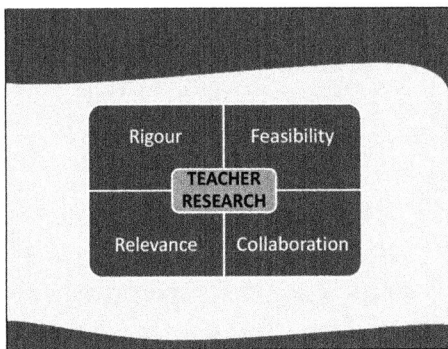

第二个作用是提供教学法，也就是让教师知道如何教学。有些教师对学科知识掌握得非常好。他们是数学天才，但是他们不知道怎样教数学。这就是培训的第二个重要作用。我们能获得教学技能。

另外，我们还可以从培训中知道该如何持续改进教学，如何进一步获得职业发展。没有接受过培训的教师没有这种意识。

我们问学生最喜欢什么样的教师，学生从来不会提到学科知识或教学技能，因为这些不是一目了然的，学生注意不到，但是它们确实存在。所以虽然我同意这些性格特点很重要，但是我觉得如果要成为好教师，只有这些是不够的。要想成为真正的好教师，你必须对学科有所洞见，同时也能很好地掌握教学技能。这些是通过培训才能获得的。

提问者 3：谢谢您，Borg 教授。我是一名英语教师，已经教了 20 年英语，所以我跟您有共通之处，您也给英语非母语的学生教英语。今天上午，陆俭明教授给外国学生教汉语。我觉得您二位在语言教学上也有相似之处。您刚才谈到教师研究有四大要点，即严谨性、可行性、相关性和合作性。不知道我的总结是否正确，但是我觉得这四个要点是针对教师研究的。那么，将汉语或英语作为外语教学是不是都要遵循这四个准则呢？这是第一个问题。

第二个问题是，今天，我们在座的大多数都是年轻教师，或是未来从事国际汉语教学工作的教师，您能不能给他们提供一些具体的建议呢？我想可能只有少部分人有五年或十年的教学经验。我们很多都不是教授。您对我们这样的教师的未来职业规划有什么具体的建议呢？

Simon Borg：第一个问题就是教师研究的标准是不是适用于不同学科。当然适用。如果和数学教师讨论教学研究，我也会谈到这四个特点。我可能会举数学方面的例子。但是总体来说，教师研究不仅限于语言教学，任何学

The second thing we get from training of course is pedagogical skill, knowing how to teach. There are also teachers who have a very good command of the subject. They are mathematical geniuses. But they don't know how to teach mathematics. So that's the second very important component of training. We get the pedagogical skill.

The other thing we get from training is an understanding of how to continue improving. We get an understanding of how to further our professional development. Teachers who haven't been trained don't get that.

When we ask pupils what they like about their teacher, pupils never mention subject matter knowledge, pedagogical skill, because those things are not directly visible to students. Students aren't aware of them. But of course they are there. So while I agree these personal characteristics are important, I disagree they are enough for someone to be an effective teacher. It's not enough for you to be really effective unless you have this good mastery of your subject, and of course a good command of pedagogical skills. That's what you get from training.

Questioner 3: Thank you Professor Borg. I have been teaching English for about 20 years. So I think I have something similar to you. Because you also teach English as a foreign language. This morning, a very famous professor, Professor Lu, has been teaching Chinese to foreign students. I think you share a similarity about teaching language to other people. My question is that, you classified teacher research into four categories: rigour, feasibility, relevance and also collaboration. I'm not sure whether my conclusion is correct or not. I think maybe these four qualities are for teachers to do research. I'm not sure whether teachers who teach Chinese or English as a foreign language, we all share the same kind of criteria. That's the first question.

My second question is, I think most of us here today, are young teachers or future teachers who teach Chinese to foreign students. So can you give us some specific advice or suggestions to use? I think only a small part of us are teachers with maybe five or ten years' experience. I think most of us here are not professors. Do you have suggestions of preparations for these teachers?

Simon Borg: So the first question is about whether these ideas about teacher research apply to different subjects. And I have no doubt they do. So if I was talking to mathematics teachers about teacher research, I would still talk about these four characteristics. The examples I give will be from mathematics perhaps. But in terms of the overall idea, teacher research is not something that is specific to language teaching. Teacher research is something that all teachers can do at any level. What

科和任何层次都适用。教师研究要让教师获益匪浅，前提是要考虑这四大要点，还要尽可能保证研究的高质量，还要确保其可行性——包括时间和其他资源的可行性，同时还要同你的工作和同事相关联，并且要与他人合作。我觉得任何学科都是如此。因此毫无疑问，从事汉语国际教育的教师都可以把这些理念完美地运用到教学过程中。

第二个问题是让我给在座的年轻教师或者未来的教师在职业发展上提出一些建议。之前我们也谈到关于教师的不同隐喻，机器人、工匠、应用科学家和反思的实践者。不管是年轻教师还是资深教师，我的建议是采用反思式模式。在这种模式下，你会不断思考你做的事情，你怎么做的，为什么这么做，效果如何，以及如何提升效率。这些是核心的问题，任何职位上的人处于任何职业阶段都应该思考。如果你是年轻教师，肯定需要更关注工作环境。如果你经验比较丰富，对整个环境的理解就比较深入。你了解教学怎么进行，比如你会更了解学生。如果你还年轻，教学经验不多，现在的理解也是有限的。经验很重要，但是教师只有经验是不够的，必须是经验加上反思。经验加反思等于专长。没有反思的经验只会让我们重复同样的工作，年复一年，毫无变化。

提问者 4：谢谢您。讲座一开始，您提到有一些师资培训效果不显著。我非常同意，因为我刚刚从美国回来。我参加了一个浸入式汉语教学的项目，专门针对青少年。我出国前接受了培训，在美国工作前也参加了几天培训。但其实，培训完后我还是不知道到底应该怎么教。我的指导教师教了我很多

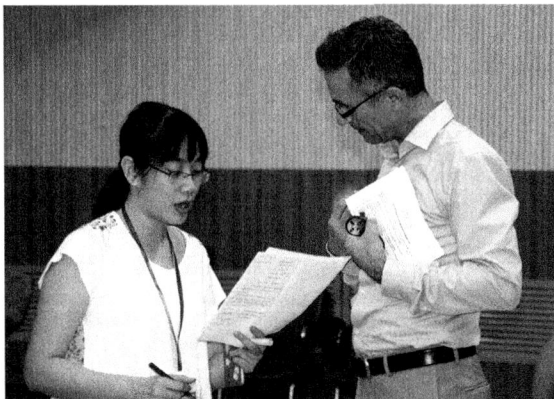

东西。我看到他们经常做游戏，经常分享，告诉学生要多和伙伴分享，而且还有很多小组活动。这种教学和中国有很大的不同，很多像我这样的新教师确实都经历过这种文化冲击。因为学生的课堂管理、教学体

we are saying here is that teacher research is more likely to be a beneficial activity for teachers when these characteristics are taken into account, when you do your best to keep the quality high, when you make sure that it is feasible, you can actually do it, given the time and other resources available, that it is relevant to your work and to your colleagues etc., and you collaborate with others, I think it is true in respective subjects. So I have no doubt that teachers who teach Chinese as a foreign language can take these ideas and use them perfectly well in your classrooms and schools.

The second question is about giving the younger members of the audience advice in terms of their career. Earlier we talked about different metaphors for teaching, the robot, the craftsperson, the applied scientist, and the reflective model. And the one I will recommend to younger and older teachers alike, or less experienced and more experienced, is the reflective model. Because if you are working with that model, it means you are constantly thinking about what you do, how you do it, why you do it, how effective it is, and how you can make it more effective. These are key questions for any professional at any stage of their career to be thinking about. When you are younger of course, you will also need to be thinking more about the context in which you work in; if you are more experienced, you have developed a good understanding of the context. You understand how things work. You have a good understanding of learners, for example. But if you are younger, you haven't yet had much experience in schools, and you won't have that kind of understanding yet. Experience is important, but you need experience plus reflection. Experience alone is not enough for a teacher to become an expert. It's experience plus reflection. Experience plus reflection equals expertise. Experience without reflection means we'll probably just go through the same routine year after year.

Questioner 4: Thank you professor for your wonderful speech. At the beginning of your lecture, you mentioned that some teacher training is useless. I can't agree more. Because I just came back from the United States. I worked in a Chinese immersion programme and taught kids. Although I have been trained before I went abroad, and I had a few days' training before I started my work. I still don't know how to start with my work exactly. My coach teacher taught me a lot. After observing, I feel like they have a lot of games, they have a lot of sharing something, like they always tell the students to share with their partner. And they have a lot of group work, which is so different from Chinese teaching. A lot of new teachers like me do experience that culture shock. Because student classroom management, education system, and the way of teaching, everything is so different.

So after teaching, I think that if we change some way of our teaching, maybe

系和教学方式，一切都大不相同。

所以，在这个项目后，我在思考能不能改变我们的教学方式，从而让教学更有效。我发现最大的问题在于学生人数。在美国，我们一个班有 27 个学生，两个教师。我们到区办公室参加培训时，大概有 20 个或 30 个教师，一个培训师。这和国内完全不一样。因为国内学生很多，但时间、教师和资源是有限的。这样，我们只能办很多场讲座让大家听听东西，但每个人学习的效果各不相同，也不能保证他们能学以致用。所以我的问题就是，有没有什么方法来改变师资培训的方式？

Simon Borg：首先把不同国家的体系进行比较是很危险的，因为每个国家的情况大不一样。您也指出了班级的规模都不一样，这是一个重要的因素。另外，教育文化也不一样。在某种程度上，即使我们让中国的班级规模变小，也不意味着教师就会用不同的方法去教学。因为不同的学习和教学方式在文化中都是根深蒂固的。这需要更多的时间才能得到改变。

您在教汉语之前接受了多少培训呢？听起来好像没有特别多，这就是问题所在，不是职业发展方面的问题，而是就职前的培训比较欠缺。教师要先接受培训，再去授课。

您还特别提到了环境的重要性。您到了一个新的环境就是一个新教师，需要花很长的时间了解当地的情况和体系。这不是通过培训能学到的事。你必须一边工作一边学，在职期间你需要有一定的空间去学习和反思。

所以比较谨慎地说，美国有很多小组活动，为什么中国不能这么做？提出这样的问题要非常谨慎，因为两个国家的情况是不同的。有些方法是适用于大规模班级的，没必要总是开展小组活动。网上有很多针对大班教学研究的文章，你可以找来看看。很多研究是针对如何教这种大班，以及如何有效照顾到全班的。

实际上教大班和教小班的策略不一样，你需要的是适用于大班的策略。有很多策略可以借鉴，因为并不是只有中国的班级规模比较大。我最近去了趟印度，那里一个班甚至有 60 个、80 个、120 个，甚至 200 个学生，这都是比较常见的。教师就需要找到教大班的方法，不可能做小组活动，而要找其他办法。

this will make the teaching more effective. I figured out the big problem is the number of students. In the United States, we have 27 students in a class with two teachers. When we go to the training in the district office, we had maybe 20 or 30 teachers with one trainer. It's just so different in Beijing. Because we have a lot of learners, but the time, the teacher and the resources are limited. In this case, we only make a lot of lectures, and introduce something, but we can't make sure everyone learns very well and they have the ability to adapt to the environment there. So my question is, is there any way to improve, to change the way of teacher training?

Simon Borg: It's always dangerous to compare systems in different countries, because the contexts vary enormously. So you gave us an example here of class size, for example, which is a very important factor. It's also educational cultures more generally. So to some extent, I think even if we make class size smaller in China for example, it does not automatically mean teachers are going to start teaching in a different way, because there are ways of teaching and ways of learning, which are very strongly established. It will take more than that. It will take more time.

How much training did you have before you start teaching Chinese the first time? Doesn't sound like you had a lot. This is the problem. It's not so much of a professional development problem. It's a pre-service training problem. People are sent into classrooms with sufficient preparation.

The other issue your story highlights is the importance of context. You go to a new context so you are a new teacher, and you need to spend quite a lot of time understanding the context, understanding how things work. That's not something that training can really prepare you for. You need to learn that on the job. And it's quite important that on the job you have some space to help you reflect about what's going on and learn.

So I'd be very cautious about saying, you know, in the USA they do lots of group work and why don't we do this in China? I'm cautious of that argument, because the contexts are very different. I think there are ways of working effectively with large groups, which don't necessarily require you to do group work or pair work all the time. If you want to read more about this, you can go online. There is quite a lot of work on teaching large classes. You can go online and search for teaching large classes. There is a lot of work on how to work effectively in large classes. There is also a lot of work on how to teach effectively in plenary sessions, in other words, when you are addressing a whole group, how to do that effectively.

It's not really that we can teach large groups using the same strategies we use in small groups. I don't think that works. What you need is strategies we can use to

所以你要非常谨慎地看待这个问题，即这么做为什么在美国行得通，在中国不行。你要知道学校情况不一样，两国的教育文化也不一样。

提问者 5：谢谢您。您讲的教师研究方面的内容令我深受启发。我是一名研究生。您能不能给我们举一些小规模教师研究的例子呢？

Simon Borg：您的问题是让我解释一下小规模研究。其实小规模研究是指你的研究对象人数不是特别多，处理的数据量也不是特别大。比如，你的班里有 50 个学生，你想做教师研究，不一定让 50 个人都参加。你可以让 5 个人参与进来，具体关注这 5 名学生的体验、兴趣以及对课程的理解。这就是小规模研究。

保持这种小规模，这样管理起来更容易。如果我说："你教 50 个学生，我希望你对每一个人进行单独的面访，每个人半个小时。"你就会说："这完全不可行，太耗时间了。"我完全同意，也绝不推荐这种做法。我会建议你面访 10 个学生，分成两组，每组 5 人。这样就可以方便管理，能做高质量的项目，不至于被太多的信息、数据和时间要求压倒。这点很重要。因为研究规模太大，有句俗语是"贪多嚼不烂"，我们做研究也一样，贪多嚼不烂。规模太大就不便于管理，你只能管理 10 个，而不是 50 个学生。不要单独面谈，而是小组面谈。如果你分析不了 500 份学生作业，就分析 20 份。这样就能更高质量地完成项目，因为研究的规模有助于保证高质量。否则，你的研究就会流于表面，因为规模太大就要研究得非常快，研究的质量也会受到影响。

只把一个学生作为研究对象也是可以的，当然你要把他作为一个案例仔细研究。因此，研究对象少也能完成高质量的研究。

work effectively with large groups. And there is plenty advice out there about how you can do that, because China is not really the only place in the world where they have large classes. I've been doing some work in India recently. And classes of 60, 80, 120, 200 students are not unusual. And teachers need to find ways how to work in those contexts. They can't do pair work. They find other ways.

So the general point is, be very careful of saying this works in the USA, why are we not doing this in China, because there are very different contexts, both the schools and the educational culture.

Questioner 5: Thank you Mr. Borg. Your lecture about teacher research is very inspiring. I'm a graduate student from a university. So I will ask you a question. Can you give me some examples of topics about small-scale research?

Simon Borg: The question is to let me explain what I mean by small-scale. Of course, small-scale in other words, means you are not working with a large number of people. You are not working with a large volume of data. For example, if you are teaching a class of 50 students, and you want to do some teacher research, you don't have to involve all 50 of them. You can work with five students. You can focus in more detail on those five, on their experience, on the work they are interested in, on their understandings. That's an example of small scale.

You are keeping it small-scale, so it's manageable. If I said to you, "Okay you teach 50 students, I'd like you to interview each of them individually, and to spend half an hour on each interview." You will say to me, "That's not feasible. It's too much." And I agree. I would never recommend that. What I would say to you is, can you interview 10 students, can you split them into two groups of five? So what we are trying to do is to manage the scale, so you are able to do a good quality project without becoming overwhelmed by too much information, too much data, too many demands on your time. This is really important. Because if it's too big, in English we have a saying, "Don't bite off more than you can chew." Don't try to do a project which is so big that you can't manage. Don't work with 50 students, work with 10. Don't do individual interviews, do group interviews. Don't try to analyse 500 pieces of students' work, analyse 20. So you can do the same work at a higher level of quality, because the scale of it allows you to. But if it's too big, your work will be superficial, because you'll have to do it quickly. And the quality will suffer as a result.

It is possible to do good research with one student. Of course you will study him or her in detail as a kind of a case study. Therefore, it is possible to do good quality research with a small number of people.

进行高质量的语言教学研究

本讲主要关注如何在语言教学中进行高质量的研究。关键问题是："我们需要做什么才能提高研究项目的质量。"这里的研究可以是你的硕士或是博士研究项目，可以是学术或者职业生涯当中任何一个研究项目。我今天要讲的和很多类型的研究都有关联。首先，如何提高研究质量？我想质量是一个非常重要的问题。如果研究的质量不高，研究的结果就不具有可信度，这一研究本身就没意义了。为了使研究结果有可信度，我们就需要在做研究时遵循一定的方式。这就是我将要讲的内容。

研究的定义

我们先来对研究进行定义，这是很好的起点，也非常重要。我在教研究

Doing Good Quality Research on Language Teaching

The focus of this session is on how to do good quality research in language teaching. Our key question is "What do we need to do to improve the quality of our research projects?". It could be your Master's or your PhD research project. It could be a research project as a part of your academic or professional career. The points I make today are relevant to many kinds of research. The focus is on how to improve the quality of research. Quality is a very important issue for us because if the research we do lacks quality, then what's the point? So if the research is not of good quality, that means we cannot trust the results. And if we can't trust the results, there is not much point in doing it. For the results to be trusted, we need to do the research in a certain way. That is what we will be talking about today.

Defining Research

Let's start with the definition of research. It's very important to have a clear definition of research. One of the problems I find sometimes when I'm teaching

方法的时候发现这样一个问题，同学们头脑当中已经对研究有了自己的定义，但这样的定义常常帮助不大。我喜欢用下面的五点来对研究进行定义。我来逐一讲一下。

规划性

首先，研究是有规划的活动。换句话说，你不能早晨醒了爬起床来说，"今天我要做些研究"，然后就去做了。这是不可能的。做研究需要有规划，我们之后会谈到这个问题。所以，研究的第一个特征就是它是有规划的行动。

系统性

第二，研究具有系统性。我们需要按照这一系统的逻辑顺序，逐一完成其中的逻辑步骤或阶段。当然，研究也有不同的方法和流程，但是一般来说，研究是系统的，其步骤有先有后。比如，需要先选题，后分析结果。一开始就分析结果是不可能的。所以，研究是系统性的过程。

目的性

第三，研究是一项有目的的活动。做研究要有非常清楚的理由。所以，如果你跟我说："我在做研究。"我就会问你："你的目的是什么？"如果你说"我不知道"，那我们就得讨论讨论了。因为研究总是有目的的。这一目的会决定你的研究问题，待会儿我们也会讲到研究问题。

到目前为止，我们讲了三点，研究是具有规划性、系统性和目的性的活动。研究总是有目的的，我们都是为了一个特定的原因而做研究。

实证性

第四，研究是实证的。"实证"这个词指的是需要收集、分析数据。我这里谈的是社会科学领域的研究，或者是语言学的研究。有些学科，如哲学，其研究主要是基于观点，并不是实证性的。但语言学和社会科学领域的研究是具有实证性的，即我们不能仅仅依靠想法，而需要收集、分析数据来进行研究。这是非常重要的一步，之后也会详细来讲。

公开性

最后，非常重要的一点是，研究是公开的，而不是私下的或个人的活动。研究的结果需要分享和公开，这就是为什么我们要出版期刊、书籍，召开会议，这样研究者能够分享他们的研究成果，其他人也可以从中学习，深入分

research methods courses is that people come to the course with a definition of research in their heads. And very often it's not a helpful definition. The definition of research I like to work with has five points. I will comment on each.

Planned

First of all, research is an activity that is planned. In other words, you can't just fall out of bed in the morning and say "Today I'm going to do some research", and you go off and do it. It's not possible. If you want to do research, you need to have a plan. We'll talk a little bit about the planning process later. So the first point to make in defining research is that it's a planned activity.

Systematic

The second point is that research is systematic. There is a logical procedure, a logical series of steps or stages that we go through. There are different ways of doing research. They have different procedures. But in general terms, research is systematic in the sense that there is a logical procedure. You need to do some things first, and then you need to do some other things a little bit later. For example, you need to choose your topic early in the process. And you need to analyse your results later in the process. It's not possible to analyse your results in the beginning, is it? So there is a system. It's a systematic process.

Purposeful

The third point in my definition is that research is a purposeful activity. What that means is that there is always a clear reason for doing it. So if you say to me, "Hey I'm doing some research" and I say "What's your purpose?" and you say "I don't know" then we'll need to talk a bit more about that, because research always has a purpose. And the purpose is what defines your research questions. We'll talk more about research questions later.

So far we've covered three points. Research is a planned activity; it's a systematic activity; and it's a purposeful activity. It's always purposeful. We are doing it for a particular reason.

Empirical

The fourth point is that research is empirical. The word "empirical" means that it involves the collection and analysis of data. I'm talking about research in the social sciences, which is the field that we are working in, or research in linguistics maybe. In some disciplines, such as philosophy, they do research which is based only on ideas. That's not empirical. In our field, linguistics and social sciences, the research we do is empirical. In other words, we don't do research just based on ideas. We are required to collect and to analyse data. That's an important part of the process. We'll talk more about that as we go along.

析这些研究成果，并在此基础之上展开进一步的研究。如果你说，"我做了一些研究，但是我没有告诉别人，还对别人保密"；我会说，"那我们用另外一个词描述你做的事吧，比如，个人的探究、反思或者学习，而不是研究，因为研究是需要分享的"。如果没有和别人分享研究成果，学科就不会进步。我们的学科就是这样发展的。

所以，研究有这五个特点，即规划性、系统性、目的性、实证性和公开性，希望大家能记住。

人们经常会说，研究就是要有统计。这种想法很常见，但却是一种误解，不一定非要有统计才能进行研究。所以，我对研究进行定义时，并没有把统计包括进来。统计只是做研究的一种方法。所以，高水平的研究不一定非要有统计。统计学本身没有错，我自己的很多研究中也会涉及统计，但是它并不是研究的必要因素。

接下来，请看下面的表述，思考一下你是否同意这些表述。

a. 有 1000 个参与者的研究比有 50 个参与者的研究好。

b. 使用统计数据的研究比不使用的研究好。

c. 只有一名参与者也可以进行研究。

d. 研究的目的是为了进行证明。

e. 研究者需要保持客观。

f. 教师可以在自己的课堂中开展高质量的研究。

g. 只要研究结果能更漂亮，研究中采取欺骗手段也是可以接受的。

我们一起来看一下。

第一条，研究规模是不是越大越好？有 1000 名参与者的研究是不是比有 50 名参与者的研究更好？我希望大家能否定这一观点。很多人从定量思维的方式出发，会同意这个观点，但我希望大家能够摒弃这种思维方式。即使一项研究有 10,000 人参与，但研究质量仍然可能很差。举例来说，我设计了一份非常糟糕的问卷，然后分发给 10,000 人，他们也都完成了问卷，我会欢呼："耶！我收回了 10,000 份问卷，我太幸运了！"但这就等同于我的研究质量高？不是，因为最基本的研究工具设计得很差，因此获得的数据质量也不高。就算我把问卷发给 100 万人也于事无补。有时我在监督学生研究时，会告诉他们："你的问卷设计得不好。"他们中有人会回答说："没

Made public

And the final point, and a very important one, is that research is a public activity, not a private or a personal activity. What that means is that the results of research need to be shared, need to be made public. That's why we have journals. That's why we have books. That's why we have conferences; so that researchers can share their results with others. And other people can learn from their results. They can look closely at those results. They can maybe build on them in future research. If you say to me, "I did some research, but I didn't tell anyone about it. I did some research, but I kept it secret just to myself", I would probably say to you, "Let's find another word to describe that. Let's call it maybe your personal inquiry, or personal reflection, or personal study, but let's not call it research, because research, by definition, needs to be shared." If no one shared their research, of course we wouldn't make any progress with our knowledge of our field. That's how our knowledge develops.

So we have five characteristics of research. Do keep them in mind. Planned, systematic, purposeful, empirical and made public.

People very often say to me, "Research means statistics." This is quite a common idea but that's a misconception. It is possible to do research without having any statistics. So that's why in my definition, it doesn't say anything about statistics, because statistics is not part of the definition of research. Statistics is just one way of doing research. So we can do good quality research without having statistics. There is nothing wrong with statistics and a lot of my own research does use numbers. But you don't have to have them. It's not a requirement.

Now please look at statements below and decide whether you agree or disagree with them.

a. Research with 1000 participants is better than research with 50.

b. Research that uses statistics is better than that which does not.

c. It is possible to do research involving only one participant.

d. The purpose of research is to prove something.

e. Researchers need to be objective.

f. Teachers can do high-quality research in their own classrooms.

g. Deception in research is acceptable if it produces better findings.

Now let's have a look at these statements.

So the first one is about size, isn't it? Is bigger better? Research with 1000 is better than research with 50. So is bigger always better when it comes to research? And I would hope you would disagree with the statement. A lot of people would agree with the statement. It's a quantitative way of thinking about research, which I would like to help you move away from. The number of participants alone does not

关系的，我可以分发给更多的人。"这是错误的想法。参与者数量多少并不能决定研究质量的高低。所以请大家否定这一观点，在做研究时，并不是规模越大越好。

第二条也是同样的道理。很多人根据自己受到的训练、接受的教育或是所处的研究环境，会认为统计学能够改进自己的研究。这也是一个误区。统计数据并不能自然而然地提高研究质量。因此，对第二个观点，希望大家也打个叉。使用统计数据的研究并非更胜一筹。我想强调，我并不是反对统计学，我自己的研究也使用统计数据。但重要的是，数据并不能自然而然地提升研究的质量。

第三条，只有一名参与者也可以进行研究。这确实是可以的，所以我们同意这个观点。即使只有一名参与者，也可以进行很高质量的研究。据我所知，有很多博士研究生就只对一名学习者或者一名教师进行非常深入的研究，这是可行的。我知道在中国，尤其是近几年，定性研究越来越普遍，但是主流还是定量研究。我知道在中国，你很难说服别人，让他们认可你的定性研究。比如期刊主编，因为这些主编都具有定量研究背景。如果你投了一篇定性研究的稿件，他们就会质疑你："怎么可能，只有五个受试者？"有时确实很难改变人们对研究的成见。所以，我们的工作就是要为自己的研究立言。你要向别人解释为什么针对一个人的研究也是高质量的。

determine the quality of your research. You can have 10,000 participants, but it is still possible to have poor quality research. I can give you an example. Let's imagine I design a questionnaire, and it's a bad questionnaire. And I give it to 10,000 people to complete. And they all complete it for me. And I could say "Yeah, Hooray! I've got 10,000 responses to my questionnaire. Lucky me". But does this make my research good quality? No, because the basic instrument that I'm using has been badly designed. And that means the data I'm getting is not good quality data. I can give it to a million people. It still wouldn't improve the quality. When I am supervising research I sometimes say "Your questionnaire isn't very well designed". The response to this sometimes is "Okay, I'll just give it to a few more people". So the thinking is that if I get more responses, that will automatically make the research better. But this is a mistake. So we cannot judge the quality of the research simply by looking at how many participants there are. So please disagree with that statement. Bigger is not automatically better when it comes to research.

And the same logic applies to the second statement. Again, a lot of people, because of their training or because of the research or educational culture they come from, believe that if you have statistics, it makes your research better. Again, this is a mistake. Having statistics doesn't automatically improve the quality of your research. Again, for second statement, please disagree with that. Research with statistics is not automatically better than studies which are not statistical. I have nothing against statistics and I do a lot of research that involves statistics myself. But it's important to remember that having numbers does not automatically make the research better quality.

The third statement in the list above is "It is possible to do research involving only one participant". It is possible. So please let's agree with that statement. It is possible to do good quality research involving one participant. I know people who have done a PhD where they studied one learner or one teacher in great detail. So it is possible to do that. I know that in China, although in recent years, qualitative research has become more common, the general tradition is still quite quantitative. And I know if you are a qualitative researcher in China, sometimes you find it difficult to persuade people that the work you are doing is of good quality. Sometimes it's difficult to persuade the editors of journals for example, because the chief editor has a very quantitative background. When you say you are doing a qualitative study, they will say "How is this possible? You only have five participants". So it is very difficult sometimes for people to change their perceptions of research. We need, therefore, to be able to defend the work we do, to explain why a study of one person can be good quality research.

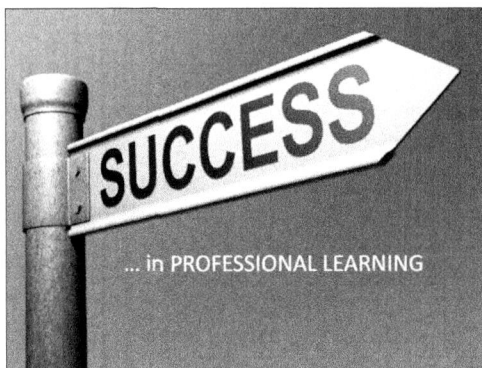

第四条，研究的目的就是为了证明。我不喜欢"证明"这个词。"证明"意味着这是最终的结论，永远不会改变。但是研究并非如此。我们在研究中会有所发现，但是通常也认可，这些发现在未来可能会改变。有人可能会进行一项新的研究，今天得到"证明"的结论可能明天就有所变化。所以我不太喜欢说证明，而是用"理解"或者"为创造知识做贡献"这样的说法。但这种贡献通常是暂时的，而不是永久的，这才是我们看待研究的正确视角。所以我不同意这个观点。

第五条，研究者需要保持客观。这点我们可以讨论很久。它的关键在于"客观"的定义。传统意义上来讲，客观指的是排除个人影响。但是，研究者本身也是人，研究总会受到一些人为影响，这是不可能完全排除的。如果客观指的是没有人为的影响，那么这个定义就有点问题。我们在研究中需要做的，就是要控制人为影响，避免过于主观。但同时也不能完全消除人为影响，因为毕竟是人在做研究。所以我对这个观点既同意也不同意，其关键在于如何定义客观。

第六条我就不多讲了，教师可以在教室中进行高质量的研究。我希望大家都同意这个观点。

第七条是关于欺骗的。一般来说，生活中的欺骗是坏事，研究中的欺骗也是坏事。我们要谈谈伦理问题。作为研究人员，我们必须要诚实。研究是一项道德活动。即使欺骗、戏弄、误导别人能产生更好的研究结果，也是不可接受的。所以一般来说，我们不能同意最后这个观点。我们不希望研究中有欺骗。

总结一下，我的回答是：a 不同意，b 不同意，c 同意，d 不同意，e 既同意也不同意，f 同意，g 不同意。

思考这些问题很有用，能够帮助我们对研究进行定义，思考什么是高质量的研究，之后我还会回顾其中几条。

The next statement is "the purpose of research is to prove something". I don't like the word "prove". It has a sense of finality—"This is the final answer forever". Of course this is not the way research works. When we do research, we have findings, but we also accept that in future those findings will change. Maybe someone else will do another study, and therefore, what seems to be "proved" today will change tomorrow. So I don't like to talk about proving something. I like to talk about understanding or making a contribution to knowledge. But that contribution is always temporary rather than permanent. That's the right way to look at research. So I disagree with this statement.

The next one says that researchers need to be objective. This is something we can talk about for a long time. The answer here depends on what you mean by "objective". Traditionally, when we say objective, we mean there is no personal influence. That's what objective means. There is no personal influence. If we think about it, if the researcher is a human being, there will always be some human influence. It's impossible to completely remove the personal influence from research that is done by humans. So this idea of objectivity meaning no personal influence is a bit problematic. So what we try to do in research is that we try to control the human influence. That's good. We don't want our research to be too subjective. But at the same time, we can't completely eliminate the human influence, because we are human researchers. So what will my answer be to this? It will be somewhere in between. I agree, but I also slightly disagree. The key to this is how we define objectivity.

We can deal with statement (f) very quickly. Of course teachers can do high-quality research in their own classrooms. I hope no one disagrees with that.

The final statement is about deception. Generally in life, deception is a bad thing. It's the same in doing research. It's not a good thing. We'll talk a little bit about ethics later on. As researchers, we have to do our best to be honest. So research is a moral activity. We have to be honest as researchers. Therefore, deception, tricking people, misleading people, is not acceptable, even if we think it will give us better results. So generally speaking, we would have to disagree with the last statement. We don't want deception in research.

So let's summarise then. My answers would be a, I disagree; b, I disagree; c, agree; d, disagree; e, I'm sort of in the middle; f, agree; and g, disagree.

Thinking about such issues is useful in helping us to define research and to think about what good quality research is and we will return to some of these points later on.

研究的层次

我们在做研究时，可以从不同的深度和抽象度层次上进行思考。请看示意图。

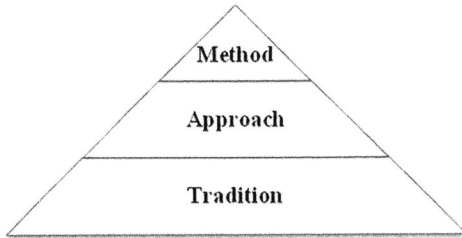

最下面一层被称为传统（有时也被称为研究范式）。我们说到的定量研究和定性研究，或者实证性研究和解释性研究，就是研究传统。中间一层是较为具体的研究过程，即研究方式，比如案例研究、实验或是调查。最上面一层最为具体，即研究方法，指的是如何收集数据，包括采访、问卷或观察等方法。所以，当大家进行研究规划的时候，可以从这三个层次考虑，即传统、方式以及方法。

定量研究和定性研究

Hammersley（2013）提到定量研究具有很多特征。我们来简要地讨论一下。

我们常常想要验证一个**假设**。假设是指我们认为正确的某一观点，比如说女孩比男孩聪明，这是一个一般性假设，即我认为这个观点是正确的。定量研究则要检验这样的假设是否正确。

定量研究使用数值类数据。定量研究之所以叫定量研究，是因为它肯定会用到数据和统计。

另外，还要强调步骤的**客观性**。例如，有控制的实验会为研究创造一个非常客观的环境。

还有就是**普遍化**。在定量研究中，我们希望得出的结论具有一定的适用性，不仅适用于我们的研究对象（被试者），而且能够适用于更大的群体。

我们也在通过定量研究寻找**关联规律**，如不同变量之间的关系、大型群

Levels of Research

When we are thinking about research it is also good to be aware that it can be discussed at different levels of depth or abstraction. Look at this diagram.

The deepest level, the bottom level is what we might call the level of tradition (this is sometimes called the research paradigm). So when we talk about quantitative research and qualitative research, or positivist and interpretive research, what we are talking there is a tradition of research. In the middle we have the approach, which is a bit more specific. So when we talk about case study or experiment or survey, that's what we call the approach. And at the top we have the most specific level, which is the method. The method is how we collect data. I might use a questionnaire; I might use interviews; I might use observation. That's the method. So when you are planning research, it's useful to think about all three levels. The tradition, the approach and the method.

Quantitative and Qualitative Research

According to Hammersley (2013), quantitative research has a number of characteristics. I will discuss these briefly.

We normally have **hypothesis** that we want to test. A hypothesis is simply a statement of what we believe to be true. My hypothesis might be that girls are smarter than boys. That's a very general hypothesis, just for the sake of example. It's a statement of what I believe to be true. Quantitative research very often tests hypothesis.

It uses numerical data. Of course, that's why it's quantitative research, because it uses numbers and statistics.

There is an emphasis on **objectivity**, the objectivity of the procedure. So, for example, controlled experiments are seen to create a very objective context for research.

There is a focus on **generalisation**. So in quantitative research, we want our results to apply, not just to the group of people we study (the sample), but to a larger population.

In quantitative research, we are also looking for **patterns of association**. We are looking for relationships between different variables, and patterns across larger groups.

In quantitative research, especially in experiments, we try to **control variables**. If you are doing an experiment, you want to control variables.

So these are characteristics of quantitative research.

Hammersley (2013) also identifies the characteristics of qualitative research. These are listed here.

体之间的比较等。

在定量研究，特别是实验中，要**控制变量**。

以上就是定量研究的特点。

Hammersley（2013）也指出了定性研究的特点，如下：

数据是没有结构的。定性研究通常会使用图片、文字、视频，而不是数字。不涉及数值型数据的研究都是定性研究。

归纳分析也是定性研究的一个重要特征，待会儿我会给大家举一个例子。

定性研究当中，**主观性**是可以接受的。定性研究总会伴随一定的主观性，要接受这一点，要重视它。当然，你不想让研究有偏颇，所以控制研究中的主观性的影响很重要。

定性研究要在**自然情景**中进行。我们不是要控制变量，而是要在自然状态下做研究。比如说，我的很多研究就需要多次到教室听课，然后描述教师在自然情景中的行为。

在定性研究中，我们倾向于研究少量的案例，而且要研究得更加详细。

最后要进行**语言分析**。通常，我们会对人们的口头话语或书面文字进行定性分析。

因此，这两种研究传统具有相反的特点。当你进行研究或是向别人介绍自己的研究时，你要清楚地说明自己的研究属于哪一个类型。

上面提到的一点是归纳思维。定性研究往往需要归纳，而定量研究往往需要演绎。两者有什么区别呢？区别在于是从具体的发现到一般的理论，还是从一般的理论到具体的发现。归纳是从具体到一般的分析过程，用于定性研究。演绎是一般到具体的分析过程，常见于定量研究。

举例来说，汉语教师进行语言教学时，对使用技术是什么态度？假如我对这个问题非常

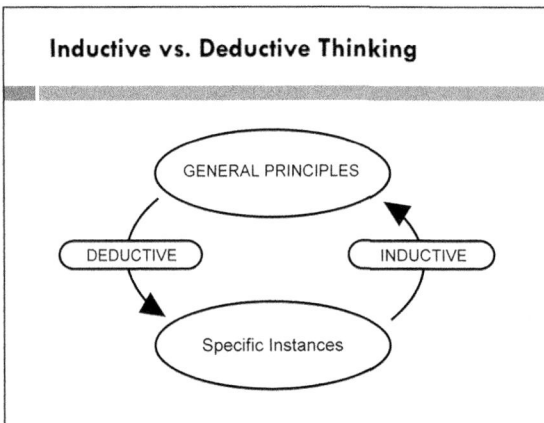

Inductive vs. Deductive Thinking

GENERAL PRINCIPLES

DEDUCTIVE

INDUCTIVE

Specific Instances

We have **unstructured data**. Unstructured, not numbers. Normally we have words, text, or maybe pictures, or videos, but not numbers. Anything that is not numerical is qualitative.

We have **inductive analysis**. This is an important characteristic of qualitative work. And I'll give an example of this below.

In qualitative research, **subjectivity** is acceptable. If you are working qualitatively, you will accept that there will always be some element of subjectivity. You accept that. That's okay. It even be valued. Of course, you do not want the research to be biased, so it is important to monitor the subjective influences on our research.

Qualitative research takes place in **natural settings**. We are not trying to control variables. We are trying to study things in natural settings. For example, a lot of the work I've done in my career has involved going to classrooms and describing what teachers do in their natural settings.

In qualitative research, we tend to work with a small number of cases that we study in greater detail.

And the last one is **verbal analysis**. Very often we are analysing what people say or write in qualitative research.

So we have these two traditions, with their contrasting characteristics. If we are starting off with a research project, it is important to think about what your position is. Or when you are presenting your research, it's important to explain what your position is.

One point mentioned above was inductive thinking. If you are working qualitatively, you will normally work inductively. If you are working quantitatively, you normally work deductively. So what is the difference? The difference is whether you go from specific findings to general theories or from general theories to specific findings. If you go from specific to general, that is inductive. And that's what we do in qualitative research. If you work from general to specific, that's the deductive way of thinking, and that's what we tend to do in quantitative research.

So let me give you an example of this. Let's say I'm interested in teachers' attitudes towards using technology for language teaching. That's the focus of my research project. I'm interested in your attitudes towards using technology in the teaching of Chinese. And I decide to interview some of you, 15, 20 of you. So what will I do? I will interview you individually. This is qualitative research. When I finish interviewing you, I will look at what you say, and I will start to arrive at some general principles from your specific examples. What are teachers' attitudes? Are they positive or negative? What are their reasons in favour or against? Those are my general categories. But where do I get them from? I start from the specific things

感兴趣，这就成了我的研究目标。我决定对 15 或者 20 位教师进行逐一面访。这属于定性研究。面访结束后，我会分析大家的话，从中归纳出若干一般性规律。比如，教师的态度是积极的还是消极的？支持或者反对利用技术的原因是什么？面访会谈得比较具体，我再从中分析，得出普遍的结论，这就是定性研究中的归纳。我们从具体的个人出发，得到普遍的结论。

Patton（2001）的书中有一幅漫画，它说明了研究中定量思维和定性思维的区别。在漫画中，一位采访者在与一位棒球选手对话。整个赛季这位棒球选手都表现很好。去年整个赛季只有两次全垒打，今年一个月就有五次。采访者问棒球选手这中间有什么差别。选手的回答是"三个"。其实这个问题是关于定性的问题，换句话说，采访者想让棒球选手解释一下其中的原因，比如说，"我改变了饮食结构，吃了很多牛排和鸡蛋"或者"我改变了训练方式"，这是访问者想要得到的答案。采访者是从定性角度提问的，但棒球选手是从定量的角度回答的，即 5-2=3。我们可以从中看出思维角度的差别。所以，在研究中定量思维和定性思维是不同的，它们就像两顶不同的帽子。如果你做定性研究，就必须要遵循定性研究的思维方式，要戴上定性研究的帽子。如果你做定性研究，又按照定量研究的方式考虑，那就麻烦了。

十年或者二十年前，研究者们还在争论是定量研究更好还是定性研究更好。现在，大家不再争论这个问题了。今天更常见的是"二者兼有"，同一个研究既用定量研究也用定性研究。这叫作"混合方法研究"。比如说，在我的研究中，我首先要发给研究对象问卷，然后再对其中一部分人进行后续访谈。我从问卷中收集定量数据，从访谈中收集定性数据，这是现在很流行的研究方法。因为两者都各有优劣，结合使用会实现更好的平衡。因此，定性和定量是可以有效结合的。

研究方式

我们不再详细地讨论这个问题。如上所述，在深层的研究传统和更加具体的研究方法之间，我们谈一谈研究方式。这里有一些研究方式的例子。

行动研究：通过行动研究，诸如一个新的教学活动被引入并被评价；

自然研究：自然研究是指研究一种现象，这种现象是在没有干扰和控制的自然情景中发生的。

that you say in your interviews. So I'm going from lots of individual interviews to some general principles at the end. This is the inductive way of working. This is how we work in qualitative research. We start from the individual specifics, and we go up to the more general principles.

In a book by Patton (2001) there is a cartoon that illustrates the differences between quantitative and qualitative thinking in research. In the cartoon, a reporter is speaking to a baseball player. The baseball player has been having a very good season – in the previous year they scored two home runs but this year they already have five. The reporter's question to the player is "What's the difference?". The player's answer is "3". The intention of the question was qualitative. In other words, the reporter wanted the baseball player to provide explanation, to say "Oh well I've changed my diet. Now I'm eating lots of eggs and steak" or "I've changed my training". That's what the interviewer was hoping for. The interviewer is thinking qualitatively, but the baseball player is thinking quantitatively. Therefore the answer is 5 minus 2 equals 3. So you can see the difference in thinking. So quantitative and qualitative ways of thinking in research are very different. It's like wearing two different hats. So if you are going to do qualitative research, you need to make sure you are thinking qualitatively with your qualitative hat on. If you are trying to do qualitative research, but you are thinking quantitatively, you are going to run into difficulties.

Ten or twenty years ago, researchers argued about whether quantitative or qualitative research was better. There is less argument today and combining both quantitative and qualitative elements has become quite common. This is called "mixed methods research". For example, for a project, I might begin with a questionnaire to a larger group, and then I might follow that up with some interviews with a smaller number of people. So quantitative data from the questionnaire, qualitative data from the interview. This is quite a popular way of doing research today. And the argument here is that they can balance each other, because they both have strengths and weakness. So qualitative and quantitative can be effectively combined.

Approaches to Research

I am not going to discuss this issue in detail. As I explained above, between the deeper level of research tradition and the more specific level of research methods, we can talk about the research approaches. Here are some examples of research approaches.

Action research, through which an intervention is introduced (such as a new teaching activity) and evaluated;

Naturalistic research, which studies phenomena in their natural settings

调查研究：这种调查研究与几组调查对象的模式相关。

个案研究：个案研究详细地聚焦于单一单元，如一位教师、一位学习者或一所学校。

相关性研究：相关性研究关注几个变量之间的关联。

实验性研究：实验性研究是指在可控的环境中研究变量之间的因果关系。

研究方式层比传统层更具体，但是它仍然没有说明究竟该怎样开展研究，也没有指出研究方法是什么。

接下来，我们来讨论一下研究过程及其不同部分，具体看一下如何在每一步提高质量。我认为，研究可以分成三个阶段。第一个阶段是规划，第二个阶段是执行，第三个阶段是报告结果。

规划研究

虽然研究过程是灵活的，但是不同的步骤之间必须遵循一定的逻辑顺序。请看下面的研究步骤列表：

- 选择题目
- 回顾文献
- 明确研究问题
- 决定如何收集数据
- 招募研究参与者
- 收集数据
- 分析数据
- 解读结果
- 报告研究

其实，研究过程并不是列表所呈现的单线性的过程，但是有些环节必须安排在其他环节之前。首先，我们要有一个大概的题目，之后深入阅读。如果没有题目，是不能进行大量阅读的。所以，首先应该有一个题目，然后开始研究文献。之后，我们就会得到研究问题。我们的研究问题是从阅读文献的过程中找到的。稍后我们会多讲一点与研究问题相关的东西。然后，决定如何收集数据，招募参与者，收集、分析数据（当然，收集和分析数据可以

without intervention or control;

Survey research, which is concerned with patterns in groups of respondents;

Case study research, where there is a detailed focus on a single unit (a teacher, a learner, a school);

Correlational research, which studies associations between variables;

Experimental research, where cause-effect relationships between variables are studied in controlled contexts.

The level of approach is more concrete than the level of tradition, but it still does not define how exactly the research will be carried out and what the research methods will be.

Let's move on now to talk about the research process generally and about different parts of it. We will consider steps we can take at each stage to improve the quality of the work we do. I find it useful to break the research process down to three simple stages. The first stage is planning. The second stage is actually doing it, conducting the research. And the third stage is reporting, where we share our results.

Planning Research

Although research is a flexible process, different stages must happen in a logical order. Look at the list of steps below:

- choose a topic
- review the literature
- define research questions
- decide how to collect data
- recruit participants
- collect data
- analyse data
- interpret the results
- report the study

Research is not a linear process in the way this list suggests. But certain things must happen before others. We start off with some general sense of our topic and then we read in more detail about it. We can't really start doing a lot of reading unless we have an idea about the topic. So maybe first you have a topic, then we start looking into literature. Then we get our research questions. Our research questions follow from our reading of the literature. We'll talk a little bit more research questions shortly. Then we decide how we collect data. Then we find our participants. Then we collect the data. This is followed by data analysis (of course data collection

循环往复，不断进行）。解读数据必须在分析数据之后，而报告结果理论上来讲是我们最后做的事情（虽然你可能会在过程中报告一部分研究）。

我必须再次重复，上述清单列举了研究项目中需要完成的一系列任务，而顺序只是它们通常发生的大致顺序。不是说每一步都是彼此独立的，比如，虽然大部分阅读会在过程早期完成，但在研究的全部过程中，你都可以持续阅读，这可以影响到我们后期所做的决定。研究不是一个线性的过程。

选择题目

选择题目是一个研究项目最早期的任务之一。有些选题很好，但有些选题则千篇一律，已经过时，或者过于普通。好的研究选题有以下几个特征。

及时

好的选题要及时。很多年前，在我研究生涯之初，我对教师的做法及其原因，尤其是对研究教师的信念，非常感兴趣。我做了很多相关研究。我也很幸运，因为当时相关研究很少，所以我的研究恰逢其时。而在 24 年后的今天，对于教师信念的研究多如牛毛，所以这个选题虽然依旧重要，但不那么及时了。而语言教学中技术使用的状况，这样的选题就非常有时效性，因为有很多人对在线学习、使用 apps 学习等非常感兴趣。相反，有些选题确实是"乏味的"，人们不再觉得它们令人振奋了。

突出重点

高质量的选题要突出重点，不能泛泛而谈。如果我问你们："你们的选题是什么？"你们说"阅读"，那我就会说，"能不能具体一点，阅读这个题目太大了。"或者，如果你们说"词汇学习"，我就会等你再进一步解释。所以好的题目是聚焦式的，不能太空泛。

独创性

好的选题要有独创性。"独创性"这个词有时会让研究者担心，因为他们觉得，独创性意味着在这个宇宙当中没有任何一个人想到过这个题目。确实很难找到这样的选题。但这并不是独创性的意义。独创性有不同的定义，它可以指采取不同的视角研究现有题目，或是在新的语境中进行研究（虽然这通常不足以成为进行一项研究的理由）。定义独创性是有不同的方法的。

and analysis can happen cyclically, in recurrent phases). Interpretation must follow analysis and reporting is logically the last thing we do (although again you may be able to report on parts of your research as you go along).

I must repeat that the list above identifies the range of tasks that need to be completed during a research project and the broad order in which they usually take place. I am not saying that each stage is independent of the others; for example, while much reading occurs early in the process, we normally continue reading throughout a project and this can influence decisions we make at later stages. Research is not a linear process.

Choosing a Topic

One of the earliest tasks in a research project is choosing a topic. Some topics are good and some are just tired or unfashionable or not exciting. Here are some characteristics of a good research topic.

Timely

A good topic is timely. It's the right time for it. Many years ago, when I started my research career, I became interested in what teachers do and why. And I became particularly interested in the study of teachers' beliefs, and I did a lot of research on that. And I was lucky, because at the time, there wasn't really much work on this and people were interested, so it was a timely topic. It was the right time to be doing that kind of research. Today, 24 years later, there has been a large volume of research of teachers' beliefs. So it's still important but not timely in the same way. If you are doing research on technology in language teaching today, that's quite timely, because it's something people are very interested in, online learning or using apps or whatever. In contrast, some topics are "tired" – people do not find them exciting any more.

Focused

A good quality topic is also focused. That means it is specific and not too broad. So if I ask you "What's the topic of your research?" and you say "Reading", I would say "Can you be more specific? Reading covers so many things". Or if you say your topic is "Vocabulary learning", we would need to make that a bit more specific. So a good topic is focused, not too big.

Original

A good topic is original. The word "original" makes researchers worried sometimes, because they think it means a topic that no one else in the universe has ever thought of. It's very difficult to find a topic that no one else has ever thought of. That's not what original means. Original can mean you are taking a different perspective on an existing topic, or your study is in a context that hasn't been

相关性

高质量的题目也要具备相关性，不仅要和研究者自己相关，而且要和整个研究领域都相关。这是非常重要的，因为我们要和整个学科的读者分享研究成果。如果我们要发表自己的研究成果，那么这个选题必须是圈内读者感兴趣的。因此你必须要确保选择的题目不仅自己感兴趣，而且别人也会感兴趣。如果没有这样做，那么在后面的环节，当你试图论证研究或者发表研究报告时，就可能会遇到困难。

研究尚不充分

选题最好是目前尚无人研究，或者没有人深入研究的。不过我们要非常谨慎，因为研究不充分可能是因为别人觉得这个题目并不重要。所以你一定要谨慎，也许人们有充足的理由不去研究一个题目。因此必须要确保你的题目虽然研究并不充分，但是也很重要，不只是没有人研究。

有了高质量的选题，一切都大不相同。比如向期刊投稿时，评审的专家会首先看题目好不好，读者会不会感兴趣。这也是决定研究质量的因素之一。

回顾文献

评估研究论文质量的另一个因素是文献综述。口头报告通常没有给文献综述留出讨论的空间。但是，在书面报告里，讨论相关研究至关重要，这一部分通常出现在"文献综述"板块里。读者将会通过文献综述判断整篇论文质量的好坏，所以思考怎么做才能提高文献综述的质量很重要。

好的文献综述有以下特点。

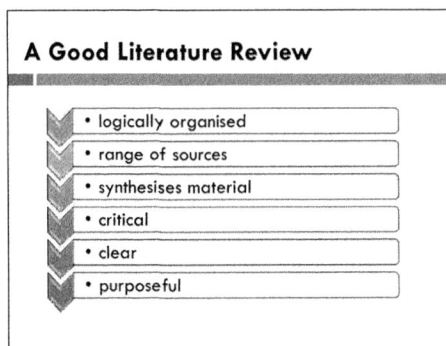

A Good Literature Review

- logically organised
- range of sources
- synthesises material
- critical
- clear
- purposeful

逻辑组织

首先，文献综述要有逻辑。当然，文献综述有不同的组织方法，可以按照话题、时间顺序或不同的研究方法来组织文献，重点是必须要有内在的逻辑（不只对作者，而且对读者也要有逻辑）。

studied before (although that is normally not enough justification for a study). There are different ways of defining originality.

Relevant

A good quality topic is also relevant. Not just relevant to the researcher, but relevant to our field. This is very important, because we are going to share the results of our research with others in the field. If we want to publish our research, it has to be of interest to a wide range of readers. So you have to make sure that you don't choose a topic that only you are interested in and no one else is. If you do that, you may have difficulties later on, when you try to justify the research or to publish it.

Under-studied

Another reason for choosing a topic is that it's under-studied. Maybe it's a topic that hasn't been studied very much. Maybe there is not much research on it. We have to be careful with this one, because sometimes a topic hasn't been studied because people don't think it's important. So you have to be careful. There may be good reasons why people haven't studied a topic. So you have to make sure that your topic is under-studied but also important. Not just under-studied.

A good quality topic does make a difference. When you send your article to a journal for example, the topic is something that people reviewing your article will look at. A good topic is a topic that readers of our journal will be interested in. That's one of the things that determines the quality of your research I think.

Reviewing the Literature

When a research paper is being reviewed, another element that influences its perceived quality is the literature review. In an oral presentation of research not much space is normally given to a discussion of the literature. But in a written paper it is important to discuss the relevant research and this normally happens in the "literature review" section. The quality of this section will influence how readers evaluate the paper, so it is important to consider what we can do to improve the quality of the literature review.

Here are some characteristics of a good literature review.

Logically organised

First of all, a literature review needs to be logically organised. There are different ways of organising it. We can organise it according to the topics; we can organise it chronologically; we could organise it according to different research methods. There are different ways of doing it. The point is that there must be some kind of logical organisation (logical to the reader, not just to the writer).

一系列资源

高质量的文献综述会参考大量的资料。如果只有在线资源，例如谷歌或其他搜索引擎中查到的内容，就不是很好。必须要引用期刊论文。文献综述应该包括期刊论文、书籍或其中章节、在线资源等，要有不同类别的资料。

最新的资源

好的文献不仅是一系列的，而且也是最新的。如果你的论文中最新的参考文献是 1992 年的，那么读者就会感到过时。也许对于有些话题，你需要参考更早的文献，但是外语教育中的大多数话题都是有新近的可参考资源的。所以，要确保引用最新的资源。

文献的整合

这点也很重要。在读文献综述的时候，我有时看到的就是一个清单，一条一条罗列了文献。好的文献综述不是这样的简单罗列，而是应该将内容进行整合，比如按照主题来组织。当然，在准备文献综述的时候，可以一条一条列出来，但之后必须要进行组织整合。好的文献综述绝对不是文献的清单。

批判性

好的文献综述要带有批判性。批判性意味着不全盘接受你阅读的所有文献，要提出质疑；你能区分出高质量和低质量的文献；批判性还意味着质疑，而不是盲目接受别人的观点。

清晰

高质量的文献综述应该是清晰的，容易理解的。

目的明确

还有一点很重要，好的文献综述应该有明确的目的。如果我问大家："你做文献综述的目的是什么？"答案不能是"我要展示我读了多少文献"，或者是"我想要告诉你我学识渊博"。必须要通过文献综述中的论证来说明你的研究是有意义的。我记得我曾经在英国评审一篇博士论文。这篇论文的文献综述非常长，有 120 页。然而读完之后，我却仍然不知道文献综述的目的是什么，作者只是单纯地总结了他阅读的文献。这就不是高质量的文献综述，因为其目的不明确。

提高研究质量的方法之一就是提高文献综述的质量。关键不在于它的篇

A range of resources

A good quality literature review will draw on a range of resources. So, for example, if I read your literature review, and you only have sources that you found online, on Google or whatever search engine, and if they are the only source you are using, that's not very good. If you haven't referred to any journal articles, that's a problem. So it is important that we use a range of sources, journal articles, books, online resources and book chapters. We need a bit of variety there.

Up-to-date

A good literature will have not only a range of resources but also be up-to-date. So if the most recent reference in your paper is 1992, the paper will feel out-of-date. Maybe for some topics you will need to rely on older sources but for most topics in foreign language education there will be recent sources to refer to. It's important that your sources are also up-to-date.

Synthesises material

This is a very important one as well. Sometimes when I read literature reviews, items are listed and discussed one by one. A literature review is not a list. You have to synthesise – that is, bring material together and organise it in some way, for example by topic. It's not just a list. Maybe when you are preparing it, you will start off by reviewing your sources one by one. That's okay. But then you need to bring them together. So a good literature review is not a list.

Critical

A good literature review is also critical. Critical means you don't simply accept everything that you read and that you can identify strengths and weaknesses in the materials you review. Critical also means that you can distinguish between the material which is of higher quality and that which is not. Being critical also means that your own voice comes through and you are not just summarising what others have said.

Clear

Of course, a good literature review is also clear. In other words, when you read it, it's easy to understand.

Purposeful

And very importantly, a good literature review has a clear purpose. So if I say to you "What is the purpose of your literature review?", the answer should not be "I want to show you how much reading I've done". That's not the answer. Or "I want to impress you with my knowledge". That's not the answer either. There has to be an argument. What is the argument that you are trying to make to justify your research? I remember once I was examining a PhD in the UK, and the literature review was about 120 pages long, a very long chapter. But when I got to the end of

幅。实际上，一般期刊论文也没有太多用于做文献回顾的空间。外语教学方面的大部分期刊论文长度都是 8000 词左右，文献综述长度应该是 1000 词左右，因此长度不是重点，重点是我上面谈到的方面。

研究问题

撰写研究问题也很重要。首先，确定好的研究问题并不容易。换句话说，你在最终确定问题前要打好几次草稿，要写好几个版本，还需要征求同事、导师或者其他人的意见。所以知道一些可以帮助大家评估研究问题质量的标准是很有帮助的。这里列举了一些 Bryman（2016）和 Punch（1998）的意见。

好的研究问题要非常**清晰**易懂，即当你看这些问题时，你知道它们在说什么。

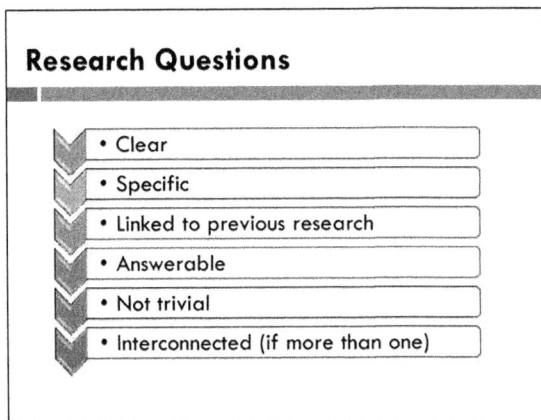

Research Questions

- Clear
- Specific
- Linked to previous research
- Answerable
- Not trivial
- Interconnected (if more than one)

好的研究问题要非常**具体**，不要太抽象和宽泛。

有时，好的研究问题还要**和以前的研究建立联系**，这样它们就有了理论背景。

好的研究问题是**能找到答案的**，这点很明显。有的问题很有意思，但是无法回答。比如，我的研究问题是："我的学生在上课的时候都在想什么？"这是非常有意思的问题，但是你无法知道它的答案。如果我说的研究问题是："全世界的汉语教师是怎么教听力的？"这也是很有意思的问题，但没有办法回答。因为我没有办法研究全世界所有的汉语教师。所以我们的问题要能找到答案。

好的研究问题**不是琐碎的**，即它不能是愚蠢的问题。我们希望这些问题是非常严肃的，因为我们要花大量时间、精力去回答这些问题。如果我的问题是"我的学生在哪里买笔"或者"我的学生们都穿多少号的鞋"，这是很清楚的问题，也可以回答，但是这些重要吗？对外语教师来说，这种问题比

it I was still not sure what the purpose was because the author never told me why they were reviewing all of that literature. So that was not a very effective literature review because it did not have a clear purpose.

So another way of improving the quality of our research is improving the quality of the literature review. It is not about how long it is. In fact, when you are writing a paper for a journal, you do not have a lot of space for your literature review. For most journals in the field of foreign language education, the length of research paper is maybe 8000 words for the whole paper. So the literature review is only about 1000 words long. That's all. Just 1000 words. So it's not about length but about the other issues I discussed above.

Research Questions

Another important part of planning research is writing research questions. The first point I must make is that writing good research questions is not easy. In other words, you need to write several drafts, several versions until you arrive at the final questions. You need to get feedback from your colleagues or your supervisor or someone to help you improve your research questions. And it's good to be aware of some criteria you can use to evaluate the quality of your research questions while you are drafting them. Here are some ideas taken from Bryman (2016) and Punch (1998).

Good research questions are **clear**. In other words, when you read the question, you understand what it means.

Good research questions are **specific** – not too general or too broad.

Good research questions are **informed by or connected to previous research** – so they have some theoretical background.

Good research questions are **answerable**. Good research questions are questions that can be answered. What I mean is that some questions are interesting, but it's not possible to answer them. For example, let's say my research question is, "What are my students thinking during my lessons?" That would be very interesting to know. But is it possible to find out? No. So there are questions which are interesting, but it's very difficult or impossible to answer them. If I say, "How do all the teachers of Chinese as a foreign language in the world teach listening?" That's an interesting question, but it's not possible to answer that question. I could not study all of them. So our questions need to be answerable.

Good research questions are also **not trivial**. Trivial means not serious. We want out our questions to be serious questions, because we are going to invest a lot of time and energy and effort in order to answer them. For example, if my question is "Where do my students buy their pens?", that's a clear question. It's answerable.

较愚蠢。它不值得研究人员花
费时间和精力。

最后，如果有多个研究问
题，这些问题必须要**有联系**。
如果你的研究中有三个研究问
题，他们都必须和总的研究目
的相关。

我们来用上面的标准评估
一些研究问题。

> How can we use online learning to improve college students' writing ability?

第一个问题："我们如何利用在线学习改进大学生的写作能力？"

问题清楚吗？大家明白这个问题的意思吗？问题的措辞是清楚易懂的。

这个问题是否具体呢？不够具体。"在线学习"是什么意思？在线学习
有很多种，我们需要具体指出到底是哪种在线学习。还有，"大学生"是非
常庞大的群体。你关心的是哪一个具体的群体？比如某所大学英语专业的大
一学生，问题要更具体些。"写作能力"是什么意思？写作能力包括很多因素，
比如准确性、组织、句法、连贯性等。这里也要更具体。

这是不是很重要或者值得研究的问题？是的，因为教写作是我们工作当
中非常重要的一部分。但是这个问题需要先具体化，再被用于进一步的研究。

下一个问题："通过互联网学习好，还是通过课堂教学学习好？"

这个问题清楚易懂吗？非常清楚。

够不够具体？不够具体。"通过互联网学习"是什么意思？有很多种在
线学习的方式，我们这里需要具体指出是哪种方式，你不可能研究所有的在
线学习方法。"课堂学习"又是什么意思？课堂学习也包括不同的方式，也
需要具体指出。"学习"是什么意思，学习什么？这里也要更具体。这里讨
论的是什么样的学生？也没有说清楚。

再有，"二者哪个更好"，这也不是一个很好的问题，因为它要求我们必
须选择其中之一。而我们都知道这两种学习方法都是很有帮助的。我们无法
给出是或者否的简单回答。

下一个例子："对于学英语的大一学生来说，互联网是有益还是有害？"

这个问题有很多毛病。"互联网""大一学生""学英语"指的都是什么？

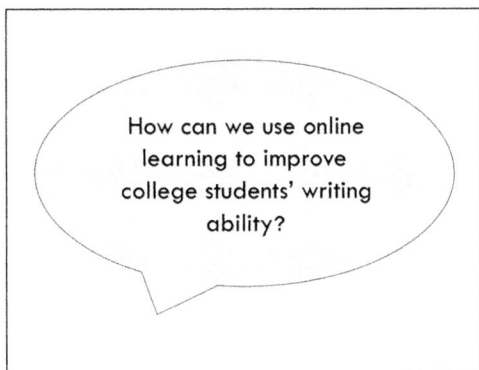

But is it an important question? For me, as a language teacher, no. It's a bit of a silly question. Or if I say, "What size of shoes do my students wear?" Again, it's possible to find the answer, but it's not the kind of question that is worth the time and effort that a researcher will invest.

One final criterion for good research questions is that, if we have more than one, they should be **inter-connected**. So if in your study you have three research questions, they should be linked in some way by the overall purpose of the study.

Now let's use the criteria above to evaluate some research questions. The first one is:

"How can we use online learning to improve college students' writing ability?"

Firstly, is it clear? Do we understand the meaning of the question? Yes. The words are clear. We understand all the words in the question.

Is it specific? No, it's not specific enough. What does "online learning" mean? There are so many different kinds of online learning. So we would need to specify which type of online learning we are interested in. And "college students", that's a very large group. Which group are we thinking about? Do we have a specific group of college students in mind – for example, first-year college students, studying English, at the university of… The students can be defined more specifically. Also, what do we mean by "writing ability"? Writing ability means so many different things. There are so many components of writing ability. We can't study all of them. Are we looking at the accuracy of writing? Are we looking at the organisation of writing? Are we looking at syntax? Are we looking at coherence? There are so many different elements of writing. So this could be made a lot more specific.

Is it an important or worthy question? Yes. Teaching writing is an important part of our work. The topic is worthy, but the question would need to be more specific before you could start developing this research further.

Let's look at another example of a research question:

"Which is better – learning through the Internet or learning through class teaching?"

Do we understand the meaning of the question? Yes, it's very clear. It's a simple question which is easy to understand.

Is it specific? No, it's not specific. What does "learning through the Internet" mean? That could mean many different things. There are many different ways of learning online or through the Internet. Again we will need to specify. We can't study every single different way of learning through the Internet. And what does "learning through class teaching" mean? Again, there are so many different ways of learning in class. You would need to specify. Also, what does "learning" mean in this question? Learning what? It's not specific enough. The students are not

而问题仅仅指出这些。我们需要聚焦于语言学习的特定方面。有益还是有害，也是属于非黑即白的提问方式。这个问题并没有经过深思熟虑，我觉得大家也没有办法回答这个问题。

最后一个例子更具体些："对于中国大学生来说，看英语电视剧会对于他们的听力有什么影响？"

这个问题比上面所有问题都更具体。它没有说看英语电视，而是说看英语电视剧。它没有说学英语，而是具体指出了"英语听力"。这是一个很好的开始，可以沿着这个思路进一步具体化。"影响"这个词很重要。假设这里研究的是因果关系，原因是看英语电视剧，结果就是提高听力。你要回答这个问题，就需要采取实验的方式。我们已经讲到了不同的研究方式。如果你想要分析因果关系，是否 A 导致了 B，就需要进行实验。例如，你需要将英语听力水平相当的学生分成两组，一组看英语电视剧，一组不看，之后测试他们的听力。当然要尽可能控制变量。这就是实验性研究方式的基本思想——比较对照组和实验组，两组唯一的差别就是他们接受的实验内容不同。

伦理

在规划阶段我们要讨论的最后一个方面是伦理。高质量的研究要符合伦理。这是什么意思呢？一般来说，它指的是研究者的行为要符合道德准则。我们要记住以下五点。

Ethics

- Obtaining informed consent
- Avoiding harm
- Maintaining confidentiality
- Maintaining anonymity
- Avoiding deception

获得知情同意

要获得参与者的明确同意，而不是强迫他们参加研究。强迫是不符合伦理的。如果我对学生说："你必须要填这个问卷，否则在我的课上你就不及格。"这就是不符合伦理的。如果我对一群教师说："你必须让我去听课，我好做研究，否则我就向校长举报你。"这也是不符合伦理的，因为我在强迫他们。在符合伦理的研

mentioned at all in the question either.

Another problem with this question is that it asks "which is better?" This is not a good question, because it's too black and white. It's like we are trying to see whether learning online is better or whether learning in class is better, whereas we know that both of them can be useful. So this kind of idea "which is better", is too black and white. I don't think we can answer questions like this in yes or no terms.

We can see similar problems in the next example of research question:

"Is the Internet helpful or harmful for freshmen in English learning?"

What do we mean by "Internet"? Which freshmen? What do we mean by "English learning"? That's everything. We need to have a focus on a particular aspect of language learning. And again, "helpful or harmful" is too black and white. It's not a very well-thought-out question and I don't think you can answer it.

Here is one final example, which is more specific.

"How does watching English TV series affect Chinese college students' English listening proficiency?"

It is more specific than those above. We have, not English TV generally, but TV series. And we've got not learning English or language, but "listening proficiency". This is a good start, and you can develop it a little bit further. The word "affect" is important in this question as it suggests that in this research the focus will be on cause and effect. The cause is watching English TV series, and the result or the effect is improving listening skills. To answer that question properly, you would need to use an experimental approach. We've already talked about different approaches to research. If you want to study cause and effect – to understand if A causes B – you need to use an experimental approach. For example, you might start with two groups of students who have similar levels of listening proficiency in English, then one group is exposed to English TV series and the other is not, then their listening is tested again. Of course, it is important to control variables as much as possible. That is the basic idea behind the experimental approach to research – comparing a control group and experimental group who differ only in terms of the treatment they receive.

Ethics

One last aspect of the planning stage of research we will discuss is ethics. Good quality research must be ethical. What do we mean by ethical? It means that as researchers we are behaving in a way that is morally correct. There are five points to keep in mind.

Obtaining informed consent

We have to make sure that the people who are participating in our research

究中，参与者都是自愿加入的，也就是"知情同意"。"同意"指的是认同或许可，"知情"指的是他们知道自己具体要做什么。所以要提供给他们需要的信息。

避免伤害

在伦理上，还要确保参与者不会受到伤害。很多年前，在心理学研究中，研究对象会被电击，然后研究者会观察他们的反应。这肯定很痛苦，也不符合伦理。在教育研究中，我们不会造成人身伤害，但是会带来心理或情感上的伤害，尴尬就是其中一种。比如我对你说："能不能让我听听你的课？"你说："可以。"然后，我偷偷把你的课录成视频，播放给别人看。这可能会让你觉得尴尬，感觉很糟。这也是不符合伦理的。不能够让别人感觉糟糕或非常尴尬，这是很重要的原则。

保密

我们还必须要保密。也就是说，我们应保护所收集信息的私密性，除非参与者允许，否则我们不能将收集到的个人信息公开。

保持匿名

通常我们要尊重别人的匿名要求，即不披露这些研究参与者的姓名或身份。我写论文的时候，可能受试对象允许我使用他们的个人信息，但是不允许我披露他们的姓名，那么，我就不能说"约翰·史密斯在这个学校教书"，我要给他们一个代号，比如说教师 A。当然，如果这位教师希望我公开他的姓名，那么只要我确定这么做不会对他造成消极影响，我就可以选择公开他的姓名。

不要欺骗

最后一点就是不要欺骗别人。比如，我想去听你的课，而且告诉你我研究的是学生，但实际上，我研究的是教师。我实际上是在骗你，这是不道德

have agreed to participate. So forcing people to participate is not ethical. If I say to my students, "You must fill in this questionnaire for me, otherwise you will fail my course.", that is not ethical. I'm forcing them to participate. If I say to a group of teachers, "You must let me observe your lessons for my research, otherwise I will report you to the principal.", that's not ethical, because I'm forcing them. So in ethical research, people participate because they want to. And we have the term "informed consent". "Consent" means agreement or permission; and "informed" means they understand what they are agreeing to. So there are two parts. They agree to participate, and also they understand what they are agreeing to. We have to give them the information they need.

Avoiding harm

To be ethical we must not cause participants any harm. Many years ago, in the field of psychology, they used to do research which involved giving people electrical shocks. That kind of research today is not ethical because it makes people suffer. In educational research, we are not going to cause people physical harm I hope. But there are other types of harm, for example, embarrassment. It's a kind of psychological or emotional harm. We must never embarrass people. For example, a teacher allows me to visit his classroom but then I video his lesson and show it to other teachers without the teacher's permission. It may be embarrassing for the teacher and he might feel bad. That's not ethical. We must never make people feel bad. We must never embarrass people. So this is an important principle.

Maintaining confidentiality

We also have to be confidential. That means the information we collect should remain private and shouldn't be shared with other people unless the participants give us permission.

Maintaining anonymity

Normally we also respect people's anonymity. In other words, you do not reveal their names or their identity. So when I write a research paper, maybe my participants give me permission to use their information but not to use their names. So I can't say "John Smith who teaches in this school". I can't reveal their names. I might give them another name or call them "Teacher 1". Of course, if the teacher wants me to use his name then I have that option as long as I am sure it will not have any negative consequences for the teacher.

Avoiding deception

The final ethical principle, which we discussed earlier, is avoiding deception. We mustn't deceive people. If I want to come to your classroom and I tell you I am studying students but I am actually studying the teacher then I'm deceiving you.

的。我们必须要诚实，这样别人才能决定是否参加我们的研究。如果我向期刊投稿，期刊的编辑要评估这篇稿件，他们也必须要看我的研究是否符合伦理标准，否则论文也不可能具有高水准。所以为了进行高水准的研究，我们必须遵循伦理要求。

我们已经讨论了规划研究阶段的不同要素。关注这些问题会提高我们的研究水准。当然，研究的水准还取决于研究活动本身——我们如何收集、分析数据。我们现在就来讨论一下这一过程。

进行研究

我们之前讲过，这个领域的研究是实证性的，也就是说我们需要收集和分析数据。我们今天没有时间讨论数据分析，但是我们可以谈谈数据收集，特别是问卷。收集数据有很多种不同方式，作为研究者，我们有责任了解这些不同的方式。下面，我给大家举例说明我们在研究项目中是如何收集数据的：

- 观察
- 采访
- 课堂讨论
- 问卷
- 绘图
- 日记 / 日志
- 照片
- 课堂文件
- 学生作业
- 考试成绩

所以从我们之前讲到的研究的三个层次来看，这是最具体的层次——研究方法。我们必须要使用能够让我们解答研究问题的方法。研究问题和数据收集方法必须要匹配。此外，一般来说，研究方法也各有优劣。例如，课堂观察可以提供教师行为的直接证据，但是比较冒昧；采访可以深入了解参与者，但是比较耗时。所以，我们务必要认识到自己使用的研究方法

That's not ethical. We have to be honest with people so they can make a decision about whether to take part in our research. Again, when you are writing a paper, presenting a paper to a journal, and the people who are evaluating your paper, will want to check that your research has been done ethically. If it's not ethical, it can't be of good quality. So in order to do a good quality research, we have to do it ethically.

We have discussed various elements in the planning stage of research. Attention to such matters will improve the quality of the work we do. But of course quality is also determined by the conduct of the study itself – how we can collect and analyse data – and we will now discuss this stage of the process.

Doing Research

As we said earlier, the research in our field is empirical, which means that we need to collect and analyse data. We do not have time to discuss analysis today, but we can discuss some aspects of data collection and look in particular at questionnaires. There are many different ways of collecting research data and it is our responsibility as researchers to be aware of all of the various options available to us. Here are some examples of how we can collect data in our projects:

- Observation
- Interviews
- Class discussions
- Questionnaires
- Drawings
- Diaries/Journals
- Photographs
- Classroom documents
- Student work
- Test scores

So in terms of the three levels of research we discussed earlier, this is the most specific level – research methods. We have to use research methods that allow us to answer our research questions. Research questions and data collection methods must match. Another general point about research methods is that each has both advantages and disadvantages. For example, classroom observation provides direct evidence of what teachers do, but it is also intrusive; and while interviews are a good way of obtaining in-depth information from respondents, they are also time-consuming. It is important for us to recognise both the strengths and the

的优势和劣势。

问卷

我们没有时间详细讨论每种研究方法，我想重点谈一谈我们收集数据时最常使用的方法之一：问卷。问卷有很多优点，Dörnyei（2003）认为，问卷省时、省力、省钱，使用方便，用途广泛。最后一点是指问卷可以被用来研究很多不同的话题。使用问卷快捷便宜，尤其当我们利用在线工具的时候更是如此。

当然，问卷也有若干劣势。Dörnyei（2003）也讨论了这些劣势。第一，问卷提供的是非常简单和肤浅的答案，"同意或者不同意""是或者否""有时或是总是"，没有具体的细节。当然问卷的设计也不是为了挖掘信息，如果你需要深入挖掘信息，使用问卷就不合适了。

第二，参与者答卷没有动力，所以他们不好好读问题，未经思考便勾选答案，每一道题都选"同意"。这些没有动力、不可靠的参与者是个难题。有时他们还跳过一些问题。回收问卷的时候，我发现有人有一半的题都没有回答。我们有时要面对这些问题，需要思考怎样解决它们。

第三，参与者的文化水平。有时他们不理解问题，所以在设计问卷的时候，语言必须简单易懂，要避免使用参与者不熟悉的术语。

第四，社会渴望度偏见。我们希望得到什么答案，参与者就倾向于给出什么答案，因为虽然这不是他们真正的想法，但是他们认为社会对这样的答案接受度更高。比如，我给大家的一个问题是："每节课教师都要备课，这非常重要。请问你是否同意？"大多数教师都会说同意，因为这是他人所期待的答案。这是社会渴望的答案，并不意味着回答"同意"

Questionnaires

- Simplicity & superficiality of answers
- Unreliable & unmotivated respondents
- Respondent literacy problems
- Social desirability bias
- Fatigue effects

(Dörnyei 2003: 10-14)

limitations of the research methods we use.

Questionnaires

We do not have time today to discuss every different research method in detail but I am going to focus on one of the most commonly-used ways of collecting data in our field: questionnaires. Questionnaires have many advantages, and Dörnyei (2003) says that questionnaires are efficient in terms of: research time, research effort, financial resources, ease of processing and versatility. The final item in this list means that questionnaires can be used to study many different topics. Questionnaires can be administered quickly and cheaply, especially if we use online tools.

Questionnaires, though, also have several disadvantages and Dörnyei (2003) discusses some of these too. First of all, they give us very simple and superficial information. We get "agree, disagree". We get "yes, no". We get "sometimes" or "always". We get quite simple, superficial information. We don't get much detail. Of course, questionnaires are not designed to get detail. If you want a lot of detail, then the questionnaire is not the right tool.

The second problem with questionnaires is that sometimes our respondents are not motivated. Therefore, they don't read the questions carefully. Or they just tick answers without thinking about the questions. Or they tick the same answer for every question. They tick "agree" for everyone. This can be a problem, unmotivated and unreliable respondents. Or they skip questions. Or they turn in the questionnaire and half of it has not been completed. We face these problems sometimes and we need to think about what we can do to address them.

The third problem with questionnaires is respondents' literacy. Sometimes respondents don't understand the questions. This means that when we design the questionnaire, we have to make sure that the language is simple or that we avoid any terminology that may be unfamiliar to respondents.

Another problem is called social desirability bias. This means that people very often give the answer that they think we want. They give the answer that they think is the most acceptable, which may not be their own personal opinions. So if I give you a statement like "It is important for teachers to plan every lesson very carefully" and ask you to agree or disagree, most teachers will choose "agree" because that is an acceptable answer. That's the socially desirable answer. It does not mean that the teachers who agree plan every lesson very carefully. Or "Smoking is a bad habit". Most people would say agree even if they smoke because that's the socially acceptable answer. This can be a problem with questionnaires. People may give you the answers they think that you want rather than their own real opinions.

的教师每节课都认真备课。或者说"抽烟是坏习惯",多数人虽然自己也抽烟,但也会同意这一观点,因为这是社会所接受的观点。问卷的问题在于,参与者会迎合社会期待,不一定说出他们的真实想法。

最后,就是疲劳的影响。由于问卷太长,人们填到一半就疲劳了,结果是他们要么不动脑筋,要么就完全放弃了。解决办法就是让问卷尽可能简短,能用 2 页就不用 4 页。我曾经收到长达 30 页的问卷,我根本就没填完,因为太长了。如果你希望参与者认真思考并回答问题,设计问卷时就必须非常谨慎,其中一点就是尽量简短。问卷说明要清晰,这样参与者更容易明白他们该怎么回答。相反,如果问卷说明含糊不清,参与者的负担就会加大,他们就更有可能会放弃。

如果你计划在研究中使用问卷,可以查阅有关研究方法的教材或是网上资源,其中确实有很多关于设计和使用问卷的有益建议。例如这是 Dunn (2013) 提出的一系列较为简单的建议:

- 问卷要简短,问题要集中。
- 避免诱导性问题。
- 不使用术语。
- 措辞和思路要符合读者的阅读水平。
- 不要把两个问题合二为一。
- 讨论敏感或有争议的问题时,要循序渐进。

我们已经讨论过其中的一些内容。如诱导性问题是指向某一特定答案或是诱导参与者给出特定回答的问题。例如,你为什么喜欢目前的工作?这个问题实际上是引导你对工作做出积极评价,但是如果你对工作不满意怎么办?这个问题就不允许这种可能性存在。所以我们设计问题的时候,不能强迫别人给出特定答案。比如,我今天做完讲座,发给大家一份反馈表,希望大家能够评价:我今天讲座的质量是非常好,棒极了,还是很出色?我给了大家三个选项,但大家没有办法对我的讲座做出负面评价。我看到结果就会认为:"太好了,大家都很满意。"有时这就是问卷的设计方式,它强迫人们给出特定的回答。"你为什么喜欢目前的工作"不是一个好问题,应该说:"你对工作的满意程度如何?"答案可以是"非常喜欢",也可以是"我讨厌这份工作",然后可以继续请参与者解释他们的答案,这样设计问卷会

The final problem with questionnaires we can mention is respondent fatigue. This happens because the questionnaire is very long and people get tired half way through, so they start answering questions without thinking or they just stop altogether. One way of addressing this issue is to keep our questionnaires as short as possible. If you can have your questionnaire on two pages, it's better than four pages. Sometimes questionnaires are ridiculously long. Someone sent me a questionnaire once. It was 30 pages long. I didn't complete it. If we want people to answer our questions carefully, we have to design our instruments well, and part of that is keeping them as short and as simple as possible. Having clear instructions also makes it easier for respondents because they will know what they are expected to do. In contrast, when the instructions on a questionnaire are unclear it creates more work for the respondents and they are more likely to give up.

If you are planning to use a questionnaire in your research, please consult research methods textbooks or online sources of advice because there is plenty of very good advice available on how to design and administer questionnaires effectively. For example, here's a simple set of recommendations from Dunn (2013):

- Keep the questionnaire short and focused.
- Avoid leading questions.
- Eliminate jargon from items.
- Match the complexity of words and ideas to the reading level of the audience.
- Do not write double-barrelled questions.
- Lead into sensitive or controversial topics gradually.

We have mentioned some of these already. A leading question is a question which suggests a particular answer or leads the respondents to answer in a particular way. For example, if I ask you this question: "Why do you like your current job?", this is a leading question because it encourages you to say positive things only. But what if you want to say negative things? The question doesn't let you. So we have to make sure that when we design our questions they don't force people to give certain answers. For example, I can give you a feedback form at the end of my lecture today. I say, "Could you please evaluate the quality of my lecture? Was it brilliant? Was it excellent? Or was it outstanding?" And I give you those three answers. I'm not really allowing you to say anything else. When I get the results, I say "Wonderful. Everyone was happy". Sometimes that's the way questionnaires are designed. They force people to give certain answers. "Why do you like your current job?" isn't a good question. It should be "How much do you like your current job?" from "I like it a lot" to "I hate it". And then "Can you explain how you feel?" That's a better way to design it.

A double-barrelled question is something like this: "How satisfied are you with

更好。

合二为一的问题是这样的：你对目前工资和工作条件满意度如何？这就是两个问题合二为一了。可能你对工资满意，对工作条件不满意，但又无法分开回答。所以这个问题问得很糟糕。我们应该分开来问。这是问卷设计中最常见的问题之一。

提高研究质量

我们谈到了提高研究质量的诸多要素，这里总结一下。

第一，确保研究有**明确的目的**。这是提高研究质量的一种方法。

第二，**有效使用文献**。前面我们讨论了一些有效文献综述的特点，请记住那些特点。

第三，确保**实验工具是经过谨慎选择和设计的**。问卷要设计好，采访问题要设计好，这都是需要时间的。

第四，确保**收集到了充分的数据**，而且这些**数据和研究问题相关**。你的研究目的是通过研究问题体现出来的，而数据能够帮助你回答这些问题。这几个因素都是相互联系的。

第五，确保分析质量也很高。无论是定性分析还是定量分析，都要**系统性地分析数据**，确保分析无误。我们今天没有讲到分析，但是分析当然也是研究过程中很重要的部分。

第六，要确保得出的**结论是建立在证据基础上的**。有时我看到有些论文的论据和论点之间没有联系。这是有问题的。结论必须有论据支撑。

第七，确保研究是符合**伦理的**。我们已经讲过了伦理原则。

第八，确保研究是**透明的**。不管是以书面形式还是以口头形式陈述你的结论，都必须要非常清晰地说明你做了什么，怎么做的，优势和挑战是什么。透明度在研究中是非常重要的，即要能够清晰详细地描述研究。

第九，整个研究过程必须是**批判性的**。不能只谈研究的优点，也要承认问题和局限性；不能盲目接受阅读的所有内容，而要明确重点，提出质疑。批判性思维是高质量研究的重要特征。

the pay and conditions of your current job?" It's two questions in one statement. Maybe you are satisfied with your pay but not satisfied with your conditions, but it is not possible to give two answers. So that's a badly designed question. It's two questions in one. We should ask two separate questions. This is one of the most common problems in questionnaire design.

Enhancing Research Quality

To conclude this session, I will now review some of the steps we can take to improve the quality of the research we do.

1. We have to make sure our research has a **clear purpose**. Make sure you have a clear purpose. That's one way of improving its quality.

2. **Make effective use of literature**. Earlier we discussed the characteristics of an effective literature review and please keep those in mind.

3. Make sure **instruments are chosen carefully and designed carefully**. If you are designing a questionnaire, design it well. If you are planning some interviews, design the questions carefully. It takes time to design good instruments.

4. Make sure that you **collect enough data** and make sure that the **data is relevant to your questions**. So your research has a purpose, the research questions relate to that purpose, and the data you collect must help you answer those questions. Everything needs to be connected.

5. Make sure the quality of the analysis is good as well. **Analyse the data systematically**, whether it's quantitative analysis or qualitative analysis. You have to make sure the analysis is done correctly. We have not covered analysis today but it is of course a very important part of the process.

6. Make sure that your **conclusions are based on the evidence** you have. Sometimes I read papers and I can't see the connection between the evidence and the conclusions. This is a problem. The conclusions must always be supported by the evidence.

7. Make sure the research is **ethical**. Earlier we talked about some ethical principles.

8. Make sure you are **transparent**. When you are presenting your research in writing, or if you are presenting it orally, make sure it's quite transparent. Being transparent means you explain clearly what you did, how you did it, what the strengths were, and what some of the challenges were. Transparency is important in research. It's about being clear and detailed in describing what we did.

9. And finally, it's important throughout the process to be **critical**. Not just to

最后，希望大家可以通过使用这些方法提高研究的质量。

*   *   *

☺ 交流互动

提问者 1：谢谢 Simon Borg 先生。我想问，英语教学中有哪些热点问题？

Simon Borg：这个问题是关于外语教学中的热点话题的。如果你阅读一些期刊论文，就会看到很多人都在研究语言学习中使用技术的方方面面，比如在线平台，等等。这显然是一个热点。另外一个话题是学习者的自主性，如何让学习者更独立地学习，这也是研究热点之一。从教学的角度来说，我刚才也讲到，很多人对教师的观点非常感兴趣。教师对语言教学的不同方面有各种观点，比如语法或阅读的观点等。语言教师对职业发展也给予越来越多的关注，我也做了很多这方面的工作。还有就是口语教学以及评估测试也是热点话题。比较简单的方法就是看看最新的期刊目录，这样就很容易知道哪些是热点话题。

提问者 2：您提到了这个领域的一些热点话题。我想问，您觉得常规研究题目和教师研究题目有什么区别呢？例如，通过文献研究或是阅读期刊可以选定常规研究题目，那语言教师怎样去选择教师研究的题目呢？

talk about the good things in our research, but also to acknowledge maybe some of the problems, some of the shortcomings. Not just to accept everything that you read, but to highlight maybe some problems and to question them. So being critical is a very important characteristic of good quality research.

I hope you can use these ideas to improve the quality of your research.

*   *   *

☺ Interaction and Communication

Questioner 1: Thank you, Mr Simon Borg. I want to ask a question. What are the hot topics in ELT?

Simon Borg: The question is about hot topics in foreign language teaching. So if you go through the academic journals and see what people are writing about, there is obviously a lot of research on technology today. That's obviously a hot topic. Different aspects of technology are used in language learning, online platforms, etc. Another topic which people continue to be interested in is learner autonomy, which is how to enable learners to learn more independently. There is a lot of research on that. From the point of view of teaching, there is a lot of interest in, as I mentioned, teachers' beliefs. The beliefs language teachers hold about different aspects of language teaching. Teachers' beliefs about teaching grammar, teachers' beliefs about teaching reading, etc. I think there is an increasing interest in professional development for language teachers. It's something I have been doing a lot of work on. And spoken language teaching and assessment are other popular topics. A good way to find out what the current issues in the field are is to look at the contents pages of recent journals. Looking through the contents pages of recent journals will give you a quick idea of what the hot topics are.

Questioner 2: You mentioned some hot topics in the field. But I'm going to ask, what do you think of the difference between the conventional research topics and teacher research topics? For example, you can choose a topic for conventional research from reading the literature or from the journal, but how do language teachers choose a topic for their teacher research?

Simon Borg: 如果你做教师研究，研究自己的教学，那么题目就要和你自己的教学经验相关。这是最重要的。你可能也受到了阅读的启发，但是它必须要和你的教学体验相关。比如遇到的教学困难或者是挑战，或者是自己教学中还不满意的地方，等等，这往往会激励教师去开展研究。学术研究的兴趣是由其他人的研究激发出来的。学术和教师研究的两个领域的选题还是存在差别的。

提问者 3：谢谢 Borg 教授！我有几个问题。第一个问题和语言教学与错误分析有关。您觉得教师是不是要熟悉学生母语的发音特点？

Simon Borg: 第一个问题，教师是不是需要或必须熟悉学生的母语发音。我们假设教师和学生讲的语言是不一样的，如果教师熟悉学生母语的发音特点，是会有帮助的。但是实际上，不是总有这种可能。我教语言的时候，有的学生是多语的，一个班里面可能有六七个不同国籍的学生，我不可能熟悉所有学生的母语。如果教师熟悉学生的母语，这肯定是一个教学优势。但是即使你不熟悉，也可以有效进行教学。

提问者 3：但是如果说教师不了解学生的母语发音，又怎么知道学生是否发音错误？如果不熟悉学生母语的发音特点，怎么能帮助他们提高？

Simon Borg: 我确认一下你的问题，即如果教师不熟悉学生的语言特点，怎么帮助他们发音。如果教师会讲学生的母语，肯定是有帮助的。通常，教师不可能会讲很多种语言。即使如此，教师也仍然能够明白发音不准确的原因，可以帮助学生改进。几年以前有一本书，叫作《学习

Simon Borg: If you are doing teacher research you are studying your own teaching, so the topic will come from or relate to your own experience in the classroom. So it will be a topic that is related to your own teaching and learning experience. That's really the most important thing. Maybe it's inspired by something you read, but it will have to be relevant to your teaching and learning context. So the topic for teacher research, it may be motivated by something you read, but it must be related to your experience. Most commonly, teachers choose topics for teacher research based on their own experience, normally based on problems they are facing, or challenges they are facing in their own teaching, or something they are not very satisfied with in their own teaching. That normally is the stimulus for the topic in teacher research. In academic research, the stimulus is normally other research from the literature. So there is that difference in where the topic comes from in teacher research and in academic research.

Questioner 3: Thank you Professor Borg. Here I have some questions. The first one is about teaching languages and error analysis. Do you think that teachers will have to be familiar with the phonology of the students' languages when they are teaching?

Simon Borg: So the first question is whether I think teachers need to be or should be familiar with the students' languages. So the situation here is one where the teacher does not speak the same language as the students and the question is whether it would be helpful if they did. Of course it would be, but in practical terms, it's not always possible. When I was a language teacher, I used to teach multi-lingual groups of students. In one class, I would have 5, 6, 7 different nationalities. So it would be impossible for teachers in that context to be familiar with all of those languages. So if the teacher is familiar with the students' own language, that is clearly an advantage. But you can still teach effectively without that advantage.

Questioner 3: But if the teachers did not know the students' phonology, how could they understand the mistakes students make? If you are not familiar with the students' language, how can you improve their language?

Simon Borg: Just to make sure I understand your question. You are saying, if the teacher doesn't know the students' language, how could they help them with their pronunciation? If a teacher does know, it helps. Very often it's impossible to expect the teachers to know many languages. I still think teachers can help with their pronunciation. A teacher can still understand the source or the reasons for

者语言》(*Learner Language*)，书名记不太清楚了，是 Michael Swan 编写或撰写的。这本书的每一章都讲了一种不同的语言，教师可以了解这些语言和英语的大致区别，这是教师可以参考的资源。教师在不熟悉学生母语发音的情况下，仍然可以理解为什么学生会有某些发音的困难，我觉得这是可以做到的。但是我们可以清楚地区分两种外语教学环境。一种是师生都讲同一种语言（如世界上大多数国家教育系统），另外一种就是老师不会讲学生的语言（如世界上很多私立的 EFL 学校）。如果老师会讲学生的语言，肯定会非常有帮助。

提问者 4：在英国有很多中国留学生，其中超过 15% 是在读硕士生。您在教他们的时候遇到过什么问题吗？我指的是做研究，中国的学术研究和英国的非常不同。我不知道这种研究的模式或者是方法论在两国有什么区别。

Simon Borg：我在不同国家都教过书，我非常清楚学生会带来不同的教育文化。所以我在课程一开始，就会请学生讲一讲自己的教育文化。如果我教的是研究方法，我就让学生先来讲讲他们对于研究的现有看法。例如，中国学生常常从定量角度考虑研究。我给他们机会，让他们先表达类似的观点，然后以此为契机，逐步开拓他们的视野。我希望他们懂得研究有时是定量的，但是还有其他的可能。所以我的教学方式就是要先了解学生的背景，帮助学生了解自己的教育文化，之后带给他们一些其他视角。如果他们本身的视角不起帮助作用或者不准确，我就会帮助他们进行反思。

所以，要先给学生表达的机会，让他们讲讲自己目前的观点，然后再去改变他们。要从学生所处的位置出发，并以此为基础。这是重要的建构主义原则。

pronunciation problems without necessarily knowing the language. There was a book a few years ago called *Learner Language*, I think it was called; it might not be the exact title. It was written by Michael Swan or edited by Michael Swan. There are different chapters in this book. And each chapter talks about a different language. It gives teachers a background or just a summary of the characteristics of those languages and how they were different from English. So that maybe is a kind of resource that the teacher can refer to. I think the teacher can still understand to a certain extent, the reasons behind pronunciation problems without having very detailed understanding of the phonology of the language. I think it's still possible. But we can clearly distinguish between two kinds of foreign language education contexts: one is where the teacher and students share a language (like in most state education systems around the world) and one where the teacher does not speak the students' language (like in many private EFL schools around the world). Teachers who share a language with the students have a resource that can be very useful.

Questioner 4: I notice that a lot of Chinese students receive their studies in the UK. And over 15% Chinese students are doing their Master's degree. What problems you might come across when you teach Chinese students during your teaching? For the research, I know that Chinese academic studies are very different from those in UK. For me, I don't understand the research model or methodology between the two countries.

Simon Borg: I teach in different countries. I'm always very aware that students bring different educational cultures to the course. So what I always try to do is to give students the chance early in the course to talk about their own educational cultures. So if we are doing a course of research methods, I will always give students the chance to explain what their current views about research are. For example, if there are students from China, it's quite common that they think of research in quantitative terms. That's why I give them opportunities to express that. And then we use that as the starting point. We try to build on what they bring with them, and then I try to help them broaden their view. I help them understand that, yes, research is sometimes quantitative, but there are other possibilities. So my general approach to teaching any course is to try to understand what the students bring with them, to help students become aware of what they bring to them, and to gradually build on that to help them understand other perspectives. And if what they bring with them is maybe unhelpful or inaccurate, then again I will try to help them review that.

I think it is important to give students the chance to express their current

提问者 5：非常感谢您精彩的发言。我对于定性研究的数据分析非常感兴趣，由于大部分数据都是通过访谈收集的，那么如何在这种情况下避免分析数据时的主观性，使分析更具有说服力呢？

Simon Borg：这个问题是关于定性研究数据分析的。今天没有时间讨论数据分析的问题了。但这是研究过程中非常重要的一步，能够提高研究水准。如果是定量研究的话，必须要选对统计方法；如果是定性研究，就要知道如何做分析。这个问题就是关于定性研究数据分析的。

举例来说，假如你做了 10 个访谈，首先就要认真听一遍所有访谈，听的同时进行文字转录，之后打印出来。这样你就会对访谈内容有比较全面的了解。接下来根据转录的文字，非常仔细地找出涉及的关键话题，这个过程叫作编码。编码，就是认真阅读转录的文字从而找出不同的讨论话题。当然，你的研究课题会决定话题。假设这个访谈是关于教师对语法教学的态度的，我就需要从转录文字中寻找教师们讲述的正面或者负面的体验，对教师们的体验进行编码，再对编码进行归类。这样，开始的很多小话题就被归纳到几个大的类别中去了。每一个访谈都这样去做，这样分组类别也会进一步扩大。最后，你就有可能找到可以深入研究的类别。

这就是归纳性数据分析。如果我问你："这些类别是怎么来的？"它们

knowledge, their current views, before we start trying to change them. So start from where the students are at, and then build on that. That's an important constructivist principle.

Questioner 5: Thank you very much for your wonderful speech. I'm very interested in the qualitative data analysis. Since most of the data is collected from the interviews, when we are analysing the data, can you give some tips on how to avoid being subjective and to make it more convincing?

Simon Borg: The question is about analysing qualitative data. We didn't have much time today to talk about data analysis. Of course it's a very important part of the research process. In order to improve the quality of our work, we need to make sure that the analysis is done well. If you are doing quantitative analysis, you need to make sure that you choose the right statistical approaches. And if you are doing qualitative analysis, you need to make sure you understand how to do that. The question we have here is about analysing qualitative data.

The general approach to analyse qualitative data, we have, let's just take an example, interviews, let's say you have got 10 interviews. So the first thing you need to do is to listen to your interviews carefully. So you have a global understanding first of all of the content. Then you will take each interview, one by one, and you will normally transcribe it while you listen to it, and type it up. So you have it printed out. Then you start working through the transcript carefully, in order to find the key topics. We call this process coding. Coding, going through the transcript carefully and identifying the different topics that are being discussed. And of course the topic will depend on the topic of the research, and what you want to discuss. So let's imagine the interview or the research is about teachers' attitudes towards teaching grammar. So I will be going through the transcript and looking for what teachers say about how they feel about teaching grammar. Positive and negative. Then I'll start coding different pages. So you have to go through the interviews quite carefully, and you end up with lots of different codes, lots of different topics or sub-topics. And you need to start organising those, putting those small topics, grouping them into large categories. So lots of small topics, you start to get bigger categories. And you do that for every single interview. As you do that, your categories will grow, will develop, will evolve. Then by the end of the process, hopefully you've got some categories you work with.

This is what we mean by inductive data analysis. If I say to you, "Where do the categories come from?" Well, the categories come from the data. The categories come from the transcripts. You don't have the categories at the beginning, but you

来自数据，来自转录的文字。它们一开始并不存在。你通过分析转录文字，创建了这些类别。

我们如何让它令人信服。首先，数据分析要有系统性，然后你要能够非常清晰地解释你的分析方法。我之前讲到过"系统性数据分析"和"透明"，即当你向别人介绍自己的研究时，要非常详细地解释数据分析方法。如果你说："我收集了数据，这是结果。"读者就不知道你做了什么、是怎样从数据推导出结果的，所以必须要解释分析过程，如认真聆听访谈、进行转录、仔细阅读、编码、对编码进行分类、多次修改分类，从而最后得出这些分类结果。这样清晰透明的解释才有说服力。

提问者 6：这两天您谈到了教师研究，今天您讲了如何做定性研究和定量研究，以及二者结合的方法。我想是否不仅在语言教学中，而且在其他研究题目中，我们都可以运用这样的方法？因为现在中国大学中有很多外国留学生，越来越多留学生都是学位生，而不是短期的语言生。我们如何帮助这些留学生进行研究？教师一方面要进行自己的研究，一方面还要帮助这些留学生做研究，例如研究汉语中的广东话。正如我刚才所说，中国有许多攻读学位的学生，包括本科生和研究生。当然，如果是英语教学，他们也不会用到汉语。对于教师来说，这属于教师研究的课题。如何帮助学生解决这一问题？今天在座的有教师、教授和研究生，如何帮助他们提升语言教学水平并且做好学术研究？

Simon Borg：第一，我们确实要考虑到不同的群体。本科生和研究生要做研究，教师还有学者也需要做研究。今天谈到的这些原则许多都是普遍性原则，适用于上述这些人群，能够帮助他们提升研究质量。

第二，我觉得这些原则也适用于教育的各个领域，在教育研究、社科研究、数学、科学等不同学科都适用。我觉得在不同群体之间这些指导原则并没有太大的差别。

如果我理解正确的话，您问到中国的大学中，越来越多的留学生接受的是英语授课，教授英语的中国教师如何应对这一挑战。这个问题和研究无关，而是关于以英语为媒介的教学。这是全世界都很关注的重要课题。现在，很

create the categories by analysing the transcripts.

The question was how we can make this convincing. One way to ensure this is you do this very systematically, and then you explain very clearly what you did. And this goes back to the point I made earlier. The very last point. Well there are two points. One is about "systematic data analysis", doing the analysis carefully. And the other point is being "transparent". That means when you present your report, you make sure that you give a detailed explanation of how you did the analysis. If you say "I collected my data and here are my results" then the reader doesn't know what you did, how you got from data to results. You have to explain what you did. You have to explain this process. I listened to the interviews carefully. I transcribed them. I went through them carefully. I coded. I categorised. I revised my categories many times. And these are the categories I ended up with. You explain all of that very clearly, very transparently. And that's what makes it convincing.

Questioner 6: Yesterday and today, you talked about teacher research. And today you explained how to do quantitative and qualitative or even blended or mixed research. I'm worried whether we can apply this kind of research not only to our language teaching, but also to other kinds of research topics. Now in Chinese universities, there are so many foreign students. I think most of them, an increasing number of them are degree students, not just short-term language learners. So how can we cope with this problem? How to help our degree learners in current Chinese universities to do their research? I mean for teachers to do their own research, and also to help the students to do their research. For example research of Chinese Cantonese. Just as I mentioned, there are so many degree learners in China, both university students and graduate students. Of course in English teaching, they use English not Chinese. For teachers, this is teacher research. For teachers, of course teachers should assist their students. How to help teachers to cope with this kind of problem? And we have teachers, professors, and graduate students here today, how to improve not only their language teaching but also academic research?

Simon Borg: We have different groups of people here today to think about. We've got university students who very often need to do a research project; and we've got undergraduate students; we've got postgraduate students; we've got teachers who do research as well; we've got academic researchers. So we've got these different groups. I think many things I've talked about today can apply to all these people. The principles I've talked about today for improving the quality of research, they are relevant to undergraduates doing research projects, and to academics

多大学出于各种原因，都决定用英语来授课。几年前，中国教育部好像规定50%的课程必须用英语授课，我记不清准确的数字，这也激发了很多人对把英语作为教学媒介的兴趣。

我做了这方面的研究，从很多角度来看，这对教师来说都有很大的挑战性。首先，有的教师本身英语水平不是很高，对自己的英语也不自信，用英语教学就非常困难。所以，大学要给这些教师提供大力支持，帮助他们提高英语，否则英语授课的质量就很差。

世界各国的经验表明，即使有些课程规定用英语教学，但实际上，授课一半是用英语，一半是用本地语言。这也是事实。

简而言之，如果大学希望教师用英语教书，就必须要提供给教师们必要的支持。

提问者 7：我想帮助学生提高阅读能力，但是他们对于阅读不感兴趣。我想知道如何来激发他们的阅读兴趣，尤其是培养他们的思辨能力。目前，国际上有哪些最新的进展？您能不能提供一些建议？

Simon Borg：这是一个很好的例子。你想教阅读，但是学生不感兴趣。

doing research. These are general principles. That's the first point.

The second thing, these apply to, I think, all aspects of education. If you are studying mathematics or science, the same principles apply. They are relevant to educational research generally, possible for social science research generally as well. I wouldn't say there is too much distinction in terms of these guidelines and different groups of people.

You asked about, if I understand your question correctly, there are increasing numbers of foreign students, and therefore the courses are taught in English. And so you are asking how Chinese teachers who are teaching English can cope with that. So this is not talking about research. This is about English medium instruction, which is a big topic around the world. There are also lots of universities, lots of contexts, where universities have decided, for whatever reason, that they will teach courses in English. I think in China, there was some kind of directive from the ministry a few years ago that said, I don't know if it's 50% of the courses have to be taught in English by a certain date, I don't remember the exact number. That has stimulated a lot of interest in China in English medium instruction.

I've done some research on the English medium instruction. I know this is quite challenging very often for the lecturers for many reasons. First of all, sometimes, the lecturer's own levels of English are not very high. So the lecturers' own confidence in their English may be low. Therefore, teaching English is of course very difficult for them. So one thing we need to do is to make sure that these lecturers have good support. They need support in improving their English, and of course the university has to provide this. You can't teach courses in English if your own levels of English are not very high. You will just have courses that are taught badly.

The other thing we know from the experience around the world is that even when "officially" a course is being taught in English, what we find is that many of them are taught half in English, and half in the local language. This is probably the reality.

But I think the simple answer to your question is that if the universities want lecturers to teach in English, they have to give them the support they need to do that. That's the short answer.

Questioner 7: I want to help my students to improve their ability in reading, but they are not interested in reading. So I want to know how to arouse their interest, especially critical thinking. What is the current achievement internationally? Can you give us some tips?

Simon Borg: This is a good example. You want to teach reading, but your

或者他们貌似对阅读不感兴趣。如果我是教师，我就会问他们为什么不感兴趣。这会成为教师研究的一个项目。首先，我要努力了解学生对阅读的态度，我会问他们："你们好像对阅读不感兴趣，是吗？"提出这个问题，是因为他们可能对阅读感兴趣，但对我提供的阅读材料不感兴趣。这是开展教师研究的一个非常好的案例。我们必须要了解学生对阅读的态度及其原因。如果他们对内容不感兴趣，我就要更换内容。如果是我给他们布置的阅读作业让他们觉得枯燥或者没有挑战性，我就要调整作业布置。也可能是因为文章太长或太难，或者以上多种原因造成了学生对阅读不感兴趣。所以，我需要进一步挖掘原因，直接问他们是最简单的方式。根据我发现的问题，我再去尝试更换阅读题材、课文，调整作业，再看看结果怎样。我觉得这是一个非常好的教师研究项目，能持续研究数周。这是我的回答。

思辨能力是另外一个问题。如果学生没有批判性思维的习惯，提高他们在外语学习中的思辨能力就很困难。如果他们在其他学科上从未运用批判性思维，那么很难让他们在语言学习中这样做。这是更宏观的教育问题，很难解决。

至于阅读，我的解决办法是做一个简单的教师研究项目，这样我就可以进一步了解学生对阅读的反应。他们为什么对阅读没有兴趣以及怎样解决这个问题。我觉得这是一个很好的教师研究实例。

提问者 8：谢谢 Simon！我有两个简单的问题。我是一名研究生。我想做一项关于俄罗斯学生习得汉语四项技能的研究。第一个问题是，如果我想改善学生的发音，您有没有什么研究方法可以推荐？

Simon Borg：我不是语言学家，也不做语言学研究。我觉得你的这个研究题目很清楚，即俄罗斯学生对于汉语技能的习得，比如发音。那么，录音是一种显而易见的方法，可以收集他们的语音片段。问题是这是实验性研究吗？换句话说，你需要研究因果吗？比如说你采取了某种教学方式，如果你想要研究影响，或自然状况下他们习得汉语发音的状况，那么就需要定期收集学生的语音录音。或者你采取某些干预手段改善学生的发音，然后再进行评价。我不知道你想要研究的是哪一种情况？

students are not interested in it, or they don't seem to be interested in reading. If I were the teacher, I would say well why they are not interested. And I would answer that question from my own teacher research project. That would be my teacher research project. Why are my students not interested or why do they seem to be not interested in reading? And then I would try to find out, to understand how they feel about reading. I would ask them questions. I would ask my students. I would say to them, "It seems to me that you are not interested in reading. Is that true?" Because maybe they are interested in reading, but they are not interested in reading the kinds of material you are giving them. So I think trying to find out a bit more about why our students react in certain ways is a very good practical example of a teacher research project. So my response will be that I need to understand how my learners feel about reading, and why they feel the way they do. Maybe the topics are not interesting, then I will have to find other topics. Maybe the tasks I give them, they don't find those challenging enough or interesting, so I need to find different types of tasks. Maybe the texts are too long or too difficult. There can be lots of reasons why they are not interested in reading. So my response would be how I can find out a bit more, and asking them is the most obvious way to find out. Then depending on what I discover, to maybe experiment with different ways of teaching reading, different topics, different texts, different tasks, and see what happens. And that seems to be a nice teacher research project to keep you going for a few weeks. So that would be my response to that kind of problem.

Critical thinking is a slightly different issue. Promoting critical thinking can be difficult in a foreign language, if the students are not accustomed to thinking critically generally. So it's very difficult to make them think critically in the language classroom if they never think critically in any other subjects. So sometimes there is a broader educational problem, which is quite difficult to address.

In terms of the reading one, that would be my way of addressing that, by doing a simple teacher research project, so I can understand my students' reactions a bit more. Why do they respond negatively to reading? What are the reasons for that? And then how can we address that? I think that's a nice practical example of teacher research.

Questioner 8: Thank you Simon. I have two easy questions. I'm a post-graduate student and I want to do research. The topic is Russian students' acquisition of Chinese four skills. You know Chinese language has four skills. My first question is, I want to improve foreign students' pronunciation, do you have any suggestions of research methods to combine them together?

132

提问者 8：我想提高他们的发音。

Simon Borg：那可以考虑实验性研究，因为你需要进行干预。干预手段可以是某种教学方法或教学任务等。然后，评估学生在干预前和干预后的发音水平，要安排对照组和实验组进行比较。建议您阅读一些与您这个话题相关的实验性研究的文献。

提问者 9：谢谢 Borg 教授！我是一所国际学校的教师。我对您所说的研究并不是很擅长，但我觉得这类研究很有帮助，很有意思。您讲到在研究规划阶段，必须要先做文献综述，再确定研究问题。我的问题是，如果我没有研究问题，就很可能会阅读很多文献，却没有明确的目标，最后迷失在茫茫文献中。那应该怎么办呢？

Simon Borg：如果我们把研究步骤排序，首先要确定题目，然后做文献综述，之后确定研究问题。您说得很对，要先确定题目，再开始文献阅读，这样，题目会指引我们阅读的方向。这个题目可能会很笼统，但依然能让阅读有所侧重。随着我们进一步阅读文献，重点也就会越明确，最后就能够确定具体的研究问题。最开始必须要有研究的题目，比如，我想研究学习者的自主性，我就开始读这方面的文献，慢慢会发现值得深入研究的问题。如果我对语法教学感兴趣，我就要读这方面的文献，同时思考可能会研究的具体问题。过程就是这样。你要在开始阅读之前有一个大致的题目，随着阅读的深入，你会开始思考想要回答的具体问题。

Simon Borg: Let me try. I'm not a linguist. I don't do linguistic research. The research topic is quite clear. Russian students' acquisition of Chinese something, to improve their pronunciation, is that right? Something to do with their pronunciation. Clearly recording them is an obvious strategy you could use. You want to collect samples of their speech. And then the question is: I this going to be an experimental study? In other words, are you looking at cause and effect? So you teach in a certain way, and you want to study the impact or do you want to study the development of their pronunciation in a more naturalistic way over time, in which case you will need to record them maybe regularly over time to see. So the question is do you want to do something that's naturalistic, to study how their acquisition develops, or do you want to do a kind of intervention, where you do something specifically to try to improve their pronunciation and to evaluate that?

Questioner 8: I think I want to improve their pronunciation.

Simon Borg: So in that case, you may need to do experimental research, because you are going to intervene. So what is your intervention going to be? Your teaching method or your teaching task? You need to measure their pronunciation before and after to see if there is any difference. Ideally you will have a control group and an experimental group, so you can compare the results. Based on the brief information you gave me, you might want to read a bit about experimental research relevant to your topic.

Questioner 9: Thank you Professor Borg. I'm a teacher from an international school. I'm not good at this kind of research, but they are very helpful and interesting. In your research planning session, you mentioned that literature review should be done before planning research questions, and my question is, if I have no research questions, when I'm doing the literature review, I may feel that I'm reading a lot of literature books without a clear purpose. I will be lost in tonnes of files.

Simon Borg: So when we put the stages in order, I think we have identified the topic, do your literature review, and then define your questions. So you are perfectly correct to say we can't start reading without any sense of our topic. We will have a sense of our topic before we start reading. And that topic will guide us. So the topic is still quite general, but it gives us a focus for our reading. And that focus becomes more clearly defined as we work our way through the literature. And then at the end of the process, we have some specific research questions. Of

主持人：非常感谢 Simon Borg 教授。在两场讲座当中，Simon Borg 教授反复提到的一个词就是"及时"。我觉得，这个讲座对于国际汉语教学是非常及时的。我有两点感受。

第一，我希望更多有汉语国际教育专业的大学能够开设研究方法课。

第二，我强烈感受到越来越多的汉语教师会开展教师研究，我们必须要更自信，更有动力。

希望 Simon Borg 教授能够在不远的将来跟我们再次见面，这样我们就可以向他汇报在这次讲座之后，我们取得了什么进展，并再次向他求教。非常感谢 Simon Borg 教授！

course, we are not going to start reading widely without any sense of our topic. We must have some general sense of the topic. I'm interested in learner autonomy. So I'm going to start reading about learner autonomy. As I read that literature, I start to think about specific questions that might be worth exploring. I'm interested in grammar teaching, so I start reading about grammar teaching. And as I read, I'll start thinking about specific questions that I might want to study. That's the process. You do need to have a sense of your topic before you start reading. And then as you read, you start to think more specifically about the questions you might answer.

Host: Thank you so much, Professor Simon Borg. In these two lectures, one word Professor Borg use quite frequently is "timely". And I think the lectures are extremely timely to our profession, professionals who teach Chinese as a second language. I will walk away with two strong feelings.

First one, I hope many universities which host programmes in teaching Chinese as a second language, will offer a course on research methodology.

And the second strong feeling is that more and more Chinese language teachers will start conducting teacher research. We need to be more confident. We need to be more motivated.

So I hope we will have Professor Borg again with us in near future, and we can learn from him, from there and to report what we have done after listening to these great lectures. Thank you so much Professor Borg.

延伸阅读
Further Reading

This list includes items cited in the text as well as other sources relevant to the topics covered in the lectures.

[1] Allison, S. (2014). *Perfect teacher-led CPD.* Carmarthen, Wales: Independent Thinking Press.

[2] Altrichter, H., Feldman, A., Posch, P. & Somekh, B. (2008). *Teachers investigate their work: An introduction to action research across the professions* (2nd ed.). London: Routledge.

[3] Borg, S. (2013). *Teacher research in language teaching: A critical analysis.* Cambridge: Cambridge University Press.

[4] Borg, S. (2015). Teacher research. In C. Coombe & J. D. Brown (Eds.), *The Cambridge guide to research in language learning and teaching* (pp. 105-111). Cambridge: Cambridge University Press.

[5] Borg, S. (2016). Action research: Not just about "results". *Research Notes, 66,* 3-5. Available at http://www.cambridgeenglish.org/images/368333-research-notes-66.pdf

[6] Borg, S. (2017). Identity and teacher research. In G. Barkhuizen (Ed.), *Reflections on language teacher identity research* (pp. 126-132). London: Routledge.

[7] Broad, K. & Evans, M. (2006). *A review of literature on professional development content and delivery modes for experienced teachers.* Toronto: Canadian Ministry of Education. Available at http://www.oise.utoronto.ca/ite/UserFiles/File/AReviewofLiteratureonPD.pdf

[8] Brown, J. D. (1988). *Understanding research in second language learning: A teacher's guide to statistics and research design.* Cambridge: Cambridge University Press.

[9] Bryman, A. (2016). *Social research methods* (5th ed.). Oxford: Oxford University Press.

[10] Burns, A. (2010). *Doing action research in English language teaching: A guide for practitioners.* New York: Routledge.

[11] Burton, D. & Bartlett, S. (2005). *Practitioner research for teachers.* London: Paul Chapman.

[12] Burton, J. (2009). Reflective practice. In A. Burns & J. C. Richards (Eds.), *The Cambridge guide to second language teacher education* (pp. 298-307). Cambridge: Cambridge University Press.

[13] Campbell, A., McNamara, O. & Gilroy, P. (2004). *Practitioner research and professional development in education.* London: Paul Chapman.

[14] Cohen, L., Manion, L. & Morrison, K. (2011). *Research methods in education* (7th ed.). London: Routledge.

[15] Creswell, J. (2013). *Research design: Qualitative, quantitative, and mixed methods approaches* (4th ed.). Thousand Oaks, CA: Sage.

[16] Denscombe, M. (2010). *The good research guide for small-scale research projects* (3rd ed.). Buckingham: Open University Press.

[17] Dörnyei, Z. (2003). *Questionnaires in second language research: Construction, administration and processing.* New York: Lawrence Erlbaum Associates.

[18] Dörnyei, Z. (2007). *Research methods in applied linguistics.* Oxford: Oxford University Press.

[19] Duff, P. (2008). *Case study research in applied linguistics.* New York: Lawrence Erlbaum Associates.

[20] Dunn, D. S. (2013). *Research methods for social psychology* (2nd ed.). Hoboken, NJ: John Wiley &

Sons.

[21] Earley, P. & Porritt, V. (2009). *Effective practices in continuing professional development: Lessons from schools.* London: Institute of Education.

[22] Gillham, B. (2008). *Small-scale social survey methods.* London: Continuum.

[23] Gulamhussein, A. (2013). Teaching the teachers: Effective professional development in an era of high stakes accountability. Alexandria, VA: Center for Public Education and the National Schools Boards Association.

[24] Guskey, T. R. (2000). *Evaluating professional development.* Thousand Oaks, CA: Corwin Press.

[25] Hammersley, M. (2013). *What is qualitative research?* London: Bloomsbury Academic.

[26] Hanks, J. (2017). *Exploratory practice in language teaching.* Basingstoke: Palgrave Macmillan.

[27] Heigham, J. & Croker, R. A. (Eds.). (2009). *Qualitative research in applied linguistics.* Basingstoke: Palgrave Macmillan.

[28] Hopkins, D. (2008). *A teachers' guide to classroom research* (4th ed.). Buckingham: Open University Press.

[29] Johnston, B. (2009). Collaborative teacher development. In A. Burns & J. C. Richards (Eds.), *The Cambridge guide to second language teacher education* (pp. 241-249). Cambridge: Cambridge University Press.

[30] Kvale, S. & Brinkmann, S. (2008). *Interviews: Learning the craft of qualitative research interviewing* (2nd ed.). Thousand Oaks: Sage.

[31] Li, M. (2015). The impact of INSET on experienced EFL teacher learning: A case study in a Chinese context. PhD thesis, School of Education, University of Leeds.

[32] Loucks-Horsley, S., Stiles, K. E., Mundry, S., Love, N. & Hewson, P. W. (2010). *Designing professional development for teachers of science and mathematics* (3rd ed.). Thousand Oaks, Calif.: Corwin Press.

[33] Mackey, A. & Gass, S. M. (2011). *A guide to research methods in second language acquisition.* London: Basil Blackwell.

[34] Muijs, D., Kyriakides, L., van der Werf, G., Creemers, B., Timperley, H. & Earl, L. (2014). State of the art - teacher effectiveness and professional learning. *School Effectiveness and School Improvement, 25*(2), 231-256.

[35] Munn, P. & Drever, E. (2004). *Using questionnaires in small-scale research: A beginner's guide.* Edinburgh: The Scottish Council for Research in Education Centre.

[36] Newby, P. (2010). *Research methods for education.* Harlow: Pearson Education Limited.

[37] Nunan, D. & Bailey, K. M. (2009). *Exploring second language classroom research.* Boston: Heinle.

[38] Patton, M. Q. (2001). *Qualitative evaluation and research methods* (3rd ed.). Newbury: Sage.

[39] Punch, M. (1998). *Introduction to social research: Quantitative and qualitative approaches.* London, England: Sage.

[40] Richards, K. (2003). *Qualitative inquiry in TESOL.* Basingstoke: Palgrave.

[41] Rust, F. & Clark, C. M. (2007). *How to do action research in your classroom.* New York: Teachers Network. http://teachersnetwork.org/tnli/Action_Research_Booklet.pdf

[42] Simpson, M. & Tuson, J. (2003). *Using observations in small-scale research: A beginner's guide.* Edinburgh: The Scottish Council for Research in Education Centre.

[43] Wyatt, M. (2010). Teachers researching their own practice. *ELT Journal, 65*(4), 417-425.

[44] Yan, C. & He, C. (2014). "Short courses shouldn't be short-lived!" enhancing longer-term impact

of short English as a foreign language inset initiatives in China. *Professional Development in Education, 41*(5), 759-776.

[45] Zepeda, S. J. (2015). *Job-embedded professional development: Support, collaboration, and learning in schools.* New York: Routledge.

Blogs on teacher research, research methods and professional development also available at: http://simon-borg.co.uk/

Examples of Teacher Research

Cambridge English Action Research scheme: http://www.cambridgeenglish.org/research-and-validation/published-research/research-notes/

"Champion Teachers" project: https://englishagenda.britishcouncil.org/sites/default/files/attachments/british_council_champion_teachers_1.pdf